Daily Readings

—— *from* ——

LUTHER'S
WRITINGS

Daily Readings
from
LUTHER'S WRITINGS

Martin Luther

Selected and Edited by

Barbara Owen

Augsburg
MINNEAPOLIS

DAILY READINGS FROM LUTHER'S WRITINGS

Cover design: Eric Lecy

Library of Congress Cataloging-in-Publication Data

Luther, Martin, 1483–1546.
    [Selections. English. 1993]
    Daily readings from Luther's writings / by Martin Luther ;
selected and edited by Barbara Owen.
    p.   cm.
    Includes bibliographical references and index.
    ISBN 0-8066-2639-9 (alk. paper)
    1. Devotional calendars.   I. Owen, Barbara, 1935–   II. Title.
BV4811.L872513   1993
242'.2—dc20   93-14902
                                              CIP

The paper used in this publication meets the minimum requirements of American National Standard for Information Sciences—Permanence of Paper for Printed Library Materials, ANSI Z329.48-1984. ∞™

Manufactured in the U.S.A.   AF 9-2639

97   96   4   5   6   7   8   9   10

Contents

FOREWORD

In a "table talk" about spiritual distress Luther disclosed his commitment to daily prayer. "Whenever I happen to be prevented by the press of duties from observing my hour of prayer," he declared, "the entire day is bad for me. Prayer helps us very much and gives us a cheerful heart, not on account of any merit in the work, but because we have spoken with God and found everything in order" (*LW* 54, p. 17).

Luther viewed daily prayer as an indispensable part of Christian formation for witness in the world. Prayer was closely tied to the catechism with its decalogue, creed, and Lord's Prayer as a spiritual survival ration in the daily struggle against sin, death, and evil. Luther had learned from the apostle Paul and St. Augustine that Christian life was an interim, the meantime between the first and second coming of Christ, at times a mean and evil time.

Luther echoed an enduring ecumenical tradition when he defined prayer as "the lifting up of heart or mind to God" (*LW* 42, p. 25). The most influential medieval theologian, Thomas Aquinas, offered the same definition of prayer. But because prayer had become a work of merit in the late medieval church, Luther insisted that prayer, like doctrine, liturgy, and ethics, be an expression of faith in Christ alone. In prayer, one should give thanks for what God did in Christ and one should petition Christ to be present through the Holy Spirit as the "counselor" who consoles and strengthens the church in the world (John 14:26). Luther, therefore, saw prayer normed by the fundamental biblical insight that Christ is the only mediator of salvation without any human merit, including the work of prayer.

Barbara Owen offers an attractive collection of Luther's writings for the four seasons of the year, highlighting particular themes and concerns. This collection may help readers to begin a life of meditation and prayer and so to break new spiritual ground for a doxological life with God and with each other as the people of God on the way from earthly struggle to eternal peace.

Eric W. Gritsch, Director
Institute for Luther Studies
Gettysburg Lutheran Seminary

PREFACE

Martin Luther (1483–1546) wrote voluminously and in many voices. The voice could be tender and compassionate, blunt and bold, humorous, nurturing, and instructional. He wrote sermons, commentaries, letters to friends, relatives, and colleagues. He wrote to argue for his point of view, to explain a concept, to encourage a prince or nobleman, to tell his wife he missed her, to show his barber how to pray.

Luther's words in this volume are taken from many such sources written at various times during the reformer's busy life. They do not represent everything Luther thought on a subject, but hint at his broad area of concern. The words will sometimes console us, sometimes surprise us, make us uncomfortable, enlighten us and lift our spirits. Always they will nurture our faith as they point to Christ, reminding us that Christ is the life and the light for all people.

I have turned to Luther often in my own life—when I am glad and joyful, when I am depressed or lonely, when I feel close to God, when I wonder where God is, in the many seasons of life that occur during all seasons of the year. With Martin Luther's vigorous and positive words comes new assurance that my sins are forgiven for Christ's sake. I am whole, loved, free to be a servant. I pray that readers will find such words here too.

Barbara Owen

INTRODUCTION
The Meditations

The meditations have all been taken from the American Edition of *Luther's Works*, abbreviated here as *LW*. The *LW* volume and page numbers for each meditation are noted beneath each page of meditations. The name of the volume is noted, as in *Lectures on Romans*, or, if the volume is a collection of documents, a particular document may be noted, such as "Fourteen Consolations."

The dates for the selections, also noted, are taken from the introductory material in the various volumes of *Luther's Works*. They are included here so the reader can know the approximate time in Luther's life that he wrote or spoke the material.

The Scripture texts heading the meditations are taken from the New Revised Standard Version Bible (NRSV) unless another translation is needed to fit Luther's use of the text in the meditation. Occasionally Luther's rendering of the text is used where he has made explicit reference to words found in his translation but not in the NRSV. In the four hundred years since Luther, new discoveries about the biblical text have led the translators of the NRSV to render some passages quite differently from the way in which Luther read them. Yet many passages are remarkably similar. Scripture included in the body of the meditations is excerpted as found in the *LW* volumes. Luther often references several verses of Scripture while commenting on another. Occasionally one of these verses has been used for the Scripture heading. Thus the meditation for Fall, Week Ten, Tuesday— Hope, an excerpt from *Lectures on Galatians*, discusses a Romans passage. Similarly, the meditation for Summer, Week Eight, Wednesday—Forgiveness, an excerpt from *Lectures on Genesis,* discusses a passage from Micah.

Because Luther wrote extensively and sometimes redundantly with the tendency to go off on tangents, some selections have been abridged to delete excess material. Many have been reworked for easier reading by dividing Luther's very long sentences and paragraphs. Occasionally some paraphrasing has been necessary to make the excerpt clear in itself. However, great care has been taken not to change Luther's meaning but simply to restructure the commentary materials so that they have the flow of meditations.

"Thee" and "thou" have usually been changed to "you," and inclusive language has been used. Nevertheless, because the translation from which these meditations come is an established standard text of Luther's writings in English, it did not seem wise to make all of its language inclusive.

Some of the meditations are taken from Luther's earlier writings such as the *First Lectures on the Psalms* (1513–15), volumes 10 and 11. These are from the Luther who had not yet fully experienced the transition from medieval Catholicism to a life with a gospel of grace that cannot be earned (what Luther would later call justification through faith without the works of the law). Nevertheless, they show that Luther was already thinking about grace. After lecturing on the Psalms, Luther chose to lecture on Romans (1515–16). Luther reported that he became more "skillful" after he had also lectured on Galatians and Hebrews, but Hilton C. Oswald, editor of *LW* 25, *Lectures on Romans,* writes in his introduction, "The whole series of lectures on Romans shows Luther already 'skillful' in his understanding of the righteousness of God, even though he still moves about in much of the vocabulary and the teaching forms of his predecessors distant and near." Within the context of Luther's later work reflected in other selections in this book, these early writings can be profitably read devotionally.

The Prayers

One finds Luther's prayers throughout his writings. In letters and sermons Luther suggested how one might pray to God in certain circumstances. Prayers of benediction conclude many of his letters. His more formal prayers are collects, penned by Luther for worship, or adapted by him from old collects for use in Reformation liturgies. Many of his hymns are, in part, prayers. The prayers in this book come from such sources. In a few instances, a Luther prayer could not be found for a weekly theme. The prayers for Mary and Hope are collects from Lutheran hymnals; the prayers for Bible Study and Music are from the *Minister's Prayer Book*. These four old collects were selected because they convey thoughts Luther might have expressed.

WINTER

CHRIST ALONE

O dear Lord, God and Father, enter not into judgment against us because no one living is justified before you. Do not count it against us as a sin that we are so unthankful for your ineffable goodness, spiritual and physical, or that we stray into sin many times every day, more often than we can know or recognize. Do not look upon how good or how wicked we have been but only upon the infinite compassion which you have bestowed upon us in Christ, your dear Son. Amen.

LW 43, 197

Monday

The LORD is my shepherd, I shall not want. Psalm 23:1

In this passage you hear that you lost sheep cannot find your way to the Shepherd yourself but can only roam around in the wilderness. If Christ, your Shepherd, did not seek you and bring you back, you would simply have to fall prey to the wolf.

But now He comes, seeks, and finds you. He takes you into His flock, that is, into Christendom, through the Word and the Sacrament. He gives His life for you, keeps you always on the right path, so that you may not fall into error. You hear nothing at all about *your* powers, good works, and merits—unless you would say that it is its strength, good works, and merit when you run around in the wilderness and are defenseless and lost.

No, Christ alone is active here, merits things, manifests His power, He seeks, carries, and directs you. He earns life for you through His death. He alone is strong and keeps you from perishing, from being snatched out of His hand (John 10:28).

And for all of this you can do nothing at all but only lend your ears, hear, and with thanksgiving receive the inexpressible treasure. Learn to know well the voice of your Shepherd, follow Him and avoid the voice of the stranger.

Commentary on "Psalm 23" (1536)
LW 12, 154–57

The true light, which enlightens everyone, # Tuesday
was coming into the world.   John 1:9

Hold fast to the only Light, and pay no attention to the fact that this or that saint led an ascetic life in some rigid monastic order, that he abstained from meat and wore a hairy garment. Exalt these saints as you will, but do not venture to tell me that they are my way, my life, my light. For this they are not. Christ is the only Lamb that bears the sins of the world (John 1:29). He alone is the true Light.

Now I am very ready to praise John the Baptist's arduous and holy life, his garment of camel's hair, his drinking of water, and his eating of locusts; but I refuse to say that this is the way that leads to heaven. He himself does not bear witness to his life of privation and holiness, but he directs me to the Lord, saying (John 1:29): "Behold, the Lamb of God, who takes away the sin of the world."

Therefore the holy evangelist concludes, as though he wished to say: "If you do not want to go astray but are intent on finding the correct and certain way to heaven without fail, then set your course for this one true Light, which radiates all the brightness and glow necessary for your salvation. Otherwise we remain in the darkness and in the shadow of death. For this is the only true Light, in contrast to which all other lights which attract people to themselves and divert them from Christ are false lights and will-o'-the-wisps which lead people to danger and destruction."

Sermons on the Gospel of St. John (1537–40)
LW 22, 71–72

Wednesday

For the LORD GOD is my Strength and my Song. He has become my Salvation.
Isaiah 12:2 (Luther's translation)

Here we have proclaimed the blessings of God that make us safe from our enemies. For the Strength is my strength, the victorious power through which I have my enemies under my feet and shall trample the serpent underfoot. The Song is my psalm and the subject matter of my psalm and song. I have no one to sing and chant about but Christ, in whom alone I have everything. Him alone I proclaim, in Him alone I glory, for He has become my Salvation, that is, my victory. For thus the word "salvation" is often used in the Scriptures for "victory," as in 1 Sam. 14:45.

Our Victory is Christ, and when we boast of Christ, we shall win. Satan and the ungodly hear the Word of God not willingly but unwillingly. Yet this Word consoles and lifts up the godly who are alarmed either in the hour of death or in want and misfortune. By means of studying the Word of God, Satan is thrown out and not by means of plans made by the flesh.

Therefore, have confidence in the Holy One of Israel, that is, Christ, who is great, unconquered, yes, all things for you. Although we are earthen vessels (2 Cor. 4:7), we tread Satan underfoot in Christ. He who is in us is greater than he who is the world, as 1 John 4:4 says.

Lectures on Isaiah (ca. 1528)
LW 16, 129–31

His understanding is unsearchable.
Isaiah 40:28c

Thursday

The Hebrew word means understanding—the power and acuteness of wisdom. It is as if He were saying: "Let them be as wise and acute as they wish. I will be more than a match for them and be wise. Just stay with Me. Look at Me as you would at a mirror. In you there is death, sin, despair, destruction. In Me there is life, righteousness, consolation, and deliverance. Since My Word is everlasting, cling to it. Do not dwell on your own thoughts."

It is natural for us who are beset by sins to struggle in our own thoughts. "But you must not give place to them. Instead, drive them out by the Word. Do not pursue your own thoughts in tribulation, because then you will fall into a sea of temptation. Rather, keep thinking of Me, because there is no search of the understanding directed against you. I will be more than a match for them. They first have to overpower Me."

Lectures on Isaiah (1527–30)
LW 17, 30

Christ Alone

Friday

Jesus said to them, "I am the bread of life. Whoever comes to me will never go hungry, and whoever believes in me will never be thirsty."   *John 6:35*

Listen to what Christ says here: "I am the bread of life." He reminds us that God is the source and wellspring of life, and that no one can give life but God. You might think: "Well, how can You, the human Christ, be the Fountain of life here on earth and dispense the bread of life unless You are God?" Yes indeed, He is just that; and apart from Christ you will not find God in heaven, in hell, or in the sea.

Now if the Father is in Christ, why search for Him elsewhere? In Christ you have the bread of life. He can give you eternal life, deliver you from death, and take the devil captive. You must trust that Christ is the Fountainhead of life, and that God has poured all His gifts, His will, and eternal life into Christ and has directed us to Him. There we are to find all. If you take hold of Him, you have all, you have taken hold of the entire Godhead.

This calls for a humble and helpless, a hungry and thirsty soul, which relies on the words and seeks God nowhere but in the Christ who lies in the manger, or wherever He may be—on the cross, in Baptism, in the Lord's Supper, or in the ministry of the divine Word, or with my neighbor or brother. That is where I will find Him.

Sermons on the Gospel of St. John (1530–32)
LW 23, 55–56

ADVENT

From heav'n above to earth I come
To bear good news to ev'ry home;
Glad tidings of great joy I bring,
Where-of I now will say and sing:

"To you this night is born a child
Of Mary, chosen virgin mild;
This little child, of lowly birth,
Shall be the joy of all the earth."

Ah, dearest Jesus, holy Child,
Make Thee a bed, soft, undefiled,
Within my heart, that it may be
A quiet chamber kept for Thee.

Monday

A shoot shall come up from the stump of Jesse, and a branch shall grow out of his roots. The spirit of the LORD *shall rest on him* . . .   Isaiah 11:1-2*

A "Shoot" will bear fruit from his root. This is what he called Christ, and such is the beginning of the rising spiritual kingdom. It is obviously different from that of an earthly kingdom, where an assembly of people is provided with a king. In this case the King is born first, and then He gathers a people for Himself. At first there will be a single Sprout risen out of the root, from the old hopeless trunk, which is nevertheless watered with a divine strength.

The prophet points to the time in which the spiritual kingdom is to have its beginning, namely, when the stump of Jesse (the family of David) will be regarded as lost, so that nothing is less hoped for than that a shoot should sprout up from the root. Yet from a trunk nearly decayed a little Twig will emerge and grow up and make holy, and it will not be prevented by heat or by rain or by all the power of the air.

And the Spirit of the Lord shall rest upon Him. Now the prophet describes the forces, weapons, and gear of that King and His Kingdom. It is a truly remarkable arsenal. Accordingly, this kingdom will be powerful in goodness and joy, not in weapons, and the protection of the Holy Spirit, who was given to Christ without measure, is certainly strong enough.

Lectures on Isaiah (ca. 1528)
LW 16, 117–18

There was a man sent from God, whose name was John. He came as a witness to testify to the light, so that all might believe through him.   John 1:6, 7

Tuesday

Now Christ was to come humbly and unassumingly, without any of the show and ostentation that is so impressive, particularly to carnal minds. He was to conquer the world with His word and His miracles, not with gun or sword or physical might. For this reason it was not an angel who was sent to succeed Moses, the prophets, the priests, and the Levites as a messenger of God; it was a man, whose name was John.

John was sent by God—that is, he did not come on his own, unauthorized. He was to rap at the doors, arouse the Jews, and testify of the Lord who had been promised them, saying:

"Open your doors and gates. Your Savior, for whom you have waited so long, has arrived! Awake! Behold, the new Light is present, the Light which was with God from the beginning, which is the eternal God, and which has now become man! See to it that you do not let Him go unnoticed! This is Christ the Lord, for whom you have yearned and sighed. He is standing before your door. Yes, He is among you (John 1:26). Go out to meet Him! Receive your Lord, and accept Him! To forestall any excuse on your part that you would gladly have received Him if only you had been informed, ample announcement and testimony has been given you."

Sermons on the Gospel of St. John (1537–40)
LW 22, 43

Wednesday

A voice cries out: "In the wilderness prepare the way of the Lord; make straight in the desert a highway for our God."
Isaiah 40:3

To "prepare the way of the Lord" is to take up a new life, the divine life. For *way* in Hebrew denotes a plan of life. Our writers, however, teach that this preparation consists in confession, fasting, and other works. These are the ways of humanity. To prepare the way of the Lord means to prepare ourselves for the Lord's activity in us, so that God may help us and our life may be the life of Christ. It is the way because people ought to have a heavenly way.

But how is this way prepared? To prepare is to clear out of the way whatever will be an obstruction. This preparation is nothing else than our humbling ourselves from our arrogance and glory. Those are the chief obstacles for the hypocrites, who walk in human ways and in their own presumption and do not accept the grace of Christ. To prepare this way, however, means to walk on it naked, without merits of any kind, in the grace of God alone and with the reception of gifts by faith.

Lectures on Isaiah (1527–30)
LW 17, 8

Not to us, O LORD, not to us, but to your name give glory, for the sake of your steadfast love and your faithfulness.
Psalm 115:1

Thursday

The coming of Christ into the flesh was given out of the pure mercy of the promising God, and was neither bestowed by the merits of human nature nor denied by demerits. Nevertheless, it was necessary that preparation and disposition for receiving Him be made, as was done in the whole Old Testament through the lineage of Christ.

The fact that God promised His Son was His mercy, but that He manifested Him was His truth and faithfulness, as Micah 7:20 says: "Thou wilt show faithfulness to Jacob and mercy to Abraham, as Thou hast sworn to our fathers from the days of old." He does not say "as we have merited," but "as Thou hast sworn." Hence the fact that God made Himself our debtor is because of the Promise of Him who is merciful, not because of the worth of meritorious human nature. He required nothing but preparation, that we might be capable of this gift, as if a prince or king of the earth would promise his robber or murderer one hundred gold coins, prepared only to wait for him at the determined time and place.

First Lectures on the Psalms II (1513–15)
LW 11, 396

Friday

Let your steadfast love become my comfort according to your promise to your servant.
Psalm 119:76

God's "steadfast love" can also be understood as referring to Christ's coming into the flesh. And so it is the prayer of the prophet and the people of the old law that what he had prophesied a little earlier should come. Indeed, let this be the general rule, that wherever any verse is explained or can be explained concerning Christ's coming into the flesh, it should at the same time be explained concerning His spiritual coming to us now through grace and in the future through glory, according to which His coming is threefold.

First Lectures on the Psalms II (1513–15)
LW 11, 468

CHRIST'S FINAL COMING

Dear Lord God, awaken us so that when your Son comes we may be prepared to receive him with joy and to serve you with clean hearts; through the same your Son Jesus Christ our Lord. Amen.

LW 53, 131

Monday

For there is still a vision for the appointed time; it speaks of the end, and does not lie. If it seems to tarry, wait for it; it will surely come, it will not delay.

Habakkuk 2:3

This Habakkuk is a prophet of comfort who is to strengthen and support the people, to prevent them from despairing of the coming of Christ, however strangely things may go. This is why he uses every device and stratagem that can serve to keep strong in their hearts the faith in the promised Christ. His message is as follows.

It is indeed true that because of the people's sins the lands shall have to be destroyed by the king of Babylon. But Christ and his kingdom shall not fail to come on that account. On the contrary, the destroyer, the king of Babylon, shall have little good out of his conquest, for he too shall perish. For it is God's nature and work to help when there is need and to come in the midst of the proper season.

In the same way we must support Christians with the word of God in anticipation of the Last Day, even though it appears that Christ is delaying long and will not come. For Christ himself says that he will come when humanity least expects it—when people are building and planting, buying and selling, eating and drinking, marrying and giving in marriage (Luke 17:27-28)—in order that at least some, though not all, can be preserved in faith. For in this matter preaching and believing are essential, as we see every day.

"Preface to the Prophet Habakkuk" (1526)
LW 35, 327

Not to us, O Lord, not to us, but to your   **Tuesday**
name give glory.   *Psalm 115:1a*

God promised for the future advent "that we should lead righteous, sober, and godly lives in this present world, looking for the blessed hope" (Titus 2:12-13). For although we have led holy lives here, that is hardly a disposition and preparation for the future glory which shall be revealed in us, so much so that the apostle says (Rom. 8:18): "The sufferings of this time are not worthy to be compared [with the glory about to be revealed to us.]"

Therefore He bestows everything gratis and only on the basis of the promise of His mercy, although He wants us to be prepared for this as much as lies in us. The whole time of grace is the preparation for the future glory and the second advent. Therefore He orders us to watch, to be prepared, and wait for Him.

First Lectures on the Psalms II (1513–15)
LW 11, 397

Wednesday

He whom God has sent speaks the words of God.   John 3:34a

Therefore the ears of all the world are now glued to the mouth of this Man who is sent, of whom John says that He is to be known as the One who is sent. Thus He alone is to be acknowledged in heaven, on earth, and in hell as the One who is effective against sin and death. Now John uses all diligence to point to Him in his sermons, so that He may increase and all the prophets may decrease. Now all must lend an ear, for to hear Him is to hear God Himself.

This is of the greatest moment, for the devil sows discord and the world is ever eager for something novel and something more perfect. It turns its back on this Man. The Turk [Muslim] forsook Him, saying: "The Messiah died long ago. I have another now; don't speak to me about Him. I have studied the matter thoroughly." The Jews are still waiting for the Messiah and hoping that He will appear. Thus they all pass the Man by and either strike Him down or hope for something else.

But do not let anyone deceive you and supplant this Preacher with another who lays claim to a method of ridding you of your sin. Do not say: "He lived long ago, and He died long ago." No, say: "He was yesterday, He is today, and He remains my Savior into the grave and from the grave. He remains my Savior until the Last Day and in eternity."

Sermons on the Gospel of St. John (1537–40)
LW 22, 486

Then comes the end, when he hands over the kingdom to God the Father, after he has destroyed every ruler and every authority and power.
1 Corinthians 15:24

Thursday

And this Kingdom on earth is identical with the one which will later be in heaven, only that it is hidden now and not open to view. A coin in a purse or pocket is a genuine coin and also remains genuine when I take it out and hold it in my hand. The only difference is that it is no longer concealed. Similarly, Christ will take the treasure which is now veiled to us, who know nothing of it but what we hear and believe, and reveal it openly and before the eyes of the whole world.

But today the order reads not to see but to believe, not to comprehend it with our five senses but to disregard these and give ear solely to what God's Word tells you, until the hour comes when Christ will put an end to this and present Himself publicly in His majesty and sovereignty. Then you will see and feel what you now believe. Sin will be erased and drowned, death will be abolished and removed from view, the devil and the world will lie at your feet. Life with God will be manifest, and all will be clear before our view, as an uncovered treasure, such as we now yearn for and look forward to.

Commentary on "1 Corinthians 15" (1534)
LW 28, 125

Friday

When all things are subjected to him, then the Son himself will also be subjected to the one who put all things in subjection under him, so that God may be all in all.
1 Corinthians 15:28

Here St. Paul reverts to and concludes what he said earlier, namely, that matters will be entirely different when Christ delivers the Kingdom to the Father; faith will be changed into clear sight, the Word into the essence, dark understanding into light and bright sun. Now it is called Christ's kingdom because we live in it by faith and do not see or hear Him physically. But later, when it is no longer hidden but is revealed before all creatures and when faith ends, it will be called God's kingdom. This is what St. Paul calls delivering the Kingdom to the Father, that is, presenting us and His whole Christendom openly to the Father into eternal clarity and glory, that He Himself may reign without cloak or cover.

But Christ will nevertheless retain His rule and majesty; for He is the same God and Lord, eternal and omnipotent with the Father. But because He now reigns through His Word and Sacrament, etc., which is not seen by the world, it is called Christ's kingdom. Everything must be subject to Him, "excepting Him who put all things under Him," until the Last Day. Then He will abolish all of this and subject Himself with His entire kingdom to the Father and say to Him: "Until now I reigned with You by faith. This I deliver to You, that they may see that I am in You and You are in Me, joined together with the Holy Spirit in one divine Majesty, and that they have and enjoy visibly in You what they hitherto believed and looked forward to."

Commentary on "1 Corinthians 15" (1534)
LW 28, 141

MARY

Almighty God, as you dealt wonderfully with your servant, the blessed virgin Mary, in choosing her to be the mother of your dearly beloved Son and thus graciously made known your regard for the poor and lowly and despised, grant us grace in all humility and meekness to receive your Word with hearty faith and to rejoice in Jesus Christ, your Son, our Lord, who lives and reigns with you and the Holy Spirit, one God, now and forever. Amen.

Lutheran Worship, 107 (#92)

Monday

"My soul magnifies God, the Lord."
Luke 1:46 (Luther's translation)

These words of the tender mother of Christ express the strong ardor and exuberant joy with which all her mind and life are inwardly exalted in the Spirit. It is as if she said: "My life and all my senses float in the love and praise of God and in lofty pleasures, so that I am no longer mistress of myself. I am exalted, more than I exalt myself, to praise the Lord."

This is the experience of all those who are saturated with the divine sweetness and Spirit. They cannot find words to utter what they feel. For to praise the Lord with gladness is not a human work; it is rather a joyful suffering and the work of God alone. It cannot be taught in words but must be learned in one's own experience. Even as David says in Psalm 34:8: "Oh, taste and see that the Lord is sweet; blessed is the one that trusts in Him." He puts tasting before seeing, because this sweetness cannot be known unless one has experienced and felt it for oneself. And no one can attain to such experience unless he or she trusts in God wholeheartly when in the depths and in sore straits.

We must also give heed to Mary's last word, which is "God." She does not say, "My soul magnifies itself" or "exalts me." She does not desire herself to be esteemed. She magnifies God alone and gives all glory to God. She leaves herself out and ascribes everything to God alone, from whom she received it. She had no thought but this: if any other maiden had got such good things from God, she would be just as glad and would not grudge them to her. Indeed, she regarded herself alone as unworthy of such an honor and all others as worthy of it.

Commentary on "The Magnificat"
[Luke 1:46-55] (1521)
LW 21, 302–3, 308

"And my spirit rejoices in God my Savior."
Luke 1:47b

Tuesday

Truly, Mary sets things in their proper order when she calls God her Lord before calling Him her Savior, and when she calls Him her Savior before recounting His works. Thereby she teaches us to love and praise God for Himself alone, and in the right order, and not selfishly to seek anything at His hands. This is done when one praises God because He is good, regards only His bare goodness, and finds one's joy and pleasure in that alone. That is a lofty, pure, and tender mode of loving and praising God and well becomes this Virgin's high and tender spirit.

But the impure and perverted lovers, who are nothing else than parasites and who seek their own advantage in God, neither love nor praise His bare goodness. They have an eye to themselves and consider only how good God is to them—that is, how deeply He makes them feel His goodness and how many good things He does to them. So long as this feeling continues, they esteem Him highly, are filled with joy and sing His praises. But just as soon as He hides His face and withdraws the rays of His goodness, leaving them bare and in misery, their love and praise are at an end. They are unable to love and praise the bare, unfelt goodness that is hidden in God. By this they prove that their spirit did not rejoice in God, their Savior, and that they had no true love and praise for His bare goodness. They delighted in their salvation much more than in the Savior, in the gift more than the Giver, in the creature rather than in the Creator.

Commentary on "The Magnificat" (1521)
LW 21, 309

Mary

Wednesday

"For He has regarded the low estate of His handmaiden. For behold, henceforth all generations will call me blessed."
Luke 1:48 (Luther's translation)

Mary confesses that the foremost work God did for her was that He regarded her, which is indeed the greatest of His works, on which all the rest depend and from which they all derive. For where it comes to pass that God turns His face toward one to regard him, there is nothing but grace and salvation, and all gifts and works must follow. Thus we read in Genesis 4:4, 5 that He had regard for Abel and his offering, but for Cain and his offering He had no regard. Here is the origin of the many prayers in the Psalter—that God would lift up His countenance upon us, that He would not hide His countenance from us, that He would make His face shine upon us and the like. And that Mary herself regards this as the chief thing, she indicates by saying: "Behold, since He has regarded me, all generations will call me blessed."

Note that she does not say all generations will speak all manner of good of her, praise her virtues, exalt her virginity or her humility, or sing of what she had done. But for this one thing alone, that God regarded her, they will call her blessed. That is to give all the glory to God as completely as it can be done.

Commentary on "The Magnificat" (1521)
LW 21, 321

She adds, "And holy is His name." That is to say: "As I lay no claim to the work, neither do I to the name and fame. For the name and fame belong to Him alone who does the work. It is not proper that one should do the work and another have the fame and take the glory. I am but the workshop in which He performs His work; I had nothing to do with the work itself. No one should praise me or give me the glory for becoming the Mother of God, but God alone and His work are to be honored and praised in me. It is enough to congratulate me and call me blessed, because God used me and did His works in me."

Behold, how completely she traces all to God, lays claim to no work, no honor, no fame. She conducts herself as before, when she still had nothing of all this; she demands no higher honors than before. She is not puffed up, does not vaunt herself or proclaim with a loud voice that she is become the Mother of God. She seeks not any glory, but goes about her usual household duties, milking the cows, cooking the meals, washing pots and kettles, sweeping out the rooms, and performing the work of maidservant or housemother in lowly and despised tasks, as though she cared nothing for such great gifts and graces.

Commentary on "The Magnificat" (1521)
LW 21, 329

Friday

"I am bringing you good news of great joy for all people: to you is born this day in the city of David a Savior."
Luke 2:10-11

Mary, you did not bear this child for yourself alone. The child is not yours; you did not bring him forth for yourself, but for me, even though you are his mother, even though you held him in your arms and wrapped him in swaddling clothes and picked him up and laid him down. But I have a greater honor than your honor as his mother. For your honor pertains to your motherhood of the body of the child, but my honor is this, that you have my treasure, so that I know none, neither humans nor angels, who can help me except this child whom you, O Mary, hold in your arms.

But how many are there who shout and jump for joy when they hear the message of the angel: "To you is born this day the Savior"? Indeed, the majority look upon it as a sermon that must be preached, and when they have heard it, consider it a trifling thing, and go away just as they were before. This shows that we have neither the first nor the second faith. We do not believe that the virgin mother bore a son and that he is the Lord and Savior unless, added to this, I believe the second thing, namely, that he is *my* Savior and Lord for the angel said, "To *you* is born the Savior." When I can say: This I accept as my own, because the angel meant it for me, then, if I believe it in my heart, I shall not fail to love the mother Mary, and even more the child, and especially the Father.

"Sermon on the Afternoon of Christmas Day, Luke 2:1-14" (1530)
LW 51, 214, 216

INCARNATION

Help, dear Lord God, that we may become and remain partakers of the new birth in the flesh of your dear Son and be delivered from our old sinful birth; through the same your Son Jesus Christ our Lord. Amen.

LW 53, 132

Incarnation

Monday

And the Word became flesh and lived among us.   John 1:14a

Christ must be true God; otherwise we are damned forever. But in His humanity He must also be a true and natural son of the Virgin Mary, from whom He inherited flesh and blood as any other child does from its mother. He was conceived of the Holy Spirit according to Luke 1:35. However, Mary, the pure virgin, had to contribute of her seed and of the natural blood that coursed from her heart. From her He derived everything, except sin, that a child naturally and normally receives from its mother. This we must believe if we are not to be lost. If, as the Manichaeans [a heretical group in the third and fourth centuries] allege, He is not a real and natural man, born of Mary, then He is not of our flesh and blood. Then He has nothing in common with us; then we can derive no comfort from Him.

However, we do not let ourselves be troubled by the blasphemies which the devil speaks against Christ the Lord. We cling to the Scriptures of the prophets and apostles, who spoke as they were moved by the Holy Spirit. Their testimony about Christ is clear. He is our Brother; we are members of His body, flesh and bone of His flesh and bone.

To sum up, we must, first of all, have a Savior who can save us from the power of sin and death. This means that He must be the true, eternal God, through whom all believers in Him become righteous and are saved.

But, secondly, we must have a Savior who is also our Brother, who is of our flesh and blood. "In the beginning was the Word"; "this Word," he added later, "became flesh."

Sermons on the Gospel of St. John (1537–40)
LW 22, 23–25

He was in the world, and the world came into being through him; yet the world did not know him.   John 1:10

Tuesday

The evangelist John says here that the Word—which was from eternity, coequal with the Father in power and glory, through which all things were made, and which is also the Life and the Light of humankind—assumed human nature, was born of Mary, came into the world, dwelt among people in this temporal life, became like any other human being in all things, took the physical, human form such as yours or mine, and was cumbered with all the human frailties, as St. Paul says in Phil. 2:7. This means that He ate, drank, slept, awakened, was tired, sad, and happy. He wept and laughed, hungered, thirsted, froze, and perspired. He chatted, worked, and prayed. In brief, He required the same things for life's sustenance and preservation that any other human being does. He labored and suffered as anyone else does. He experienced both fortune and misfortune. The only difference between Him and all others was that He was sinless. Since He was also very God, He was free of sin. And yet He was the one through whom the whole world was created and made.

Sermons on the Gospel of St. John (1537–40)
LW 22, 73

Wednesday

The spirit of the Lord GOD is upon me, because the LORD has anointed me; he has sent me to bring good news to the oppressed.   Isaiah 61:1a

It is Christ who is defined here as the One to whom the office of the Word has been committed. Be content with Him, the God incarnate. Then you will remain in peace and safety, and you will know God. Cast off speculations about divine glory; stay with Christ crucified, whom Paul and others preach. But those who immerse themselves in their own speculations about the divine, for example, why God spares so many unbelievers and condemns so many, they are plunged into confusion or despair because of such speculations. Since Christ and His office are here set forth, we must be content with that description.

It is because of His humanity and His incarnation that Christ becomes sweet to us, and through Him God becomes sweet to us. Let us therefore begin to ascend step by step from Christ's crying in His swaddling clothes up to His Passion. Then we shall easily know God. I am saying this so that you do not begin to contemplate God from the top, but start with the weak elements. We should busy ourselves completely with treating, knowing, and considering this man. Then you will know that He is the Way, the Truth, and the Life (John 14:6). So He set forth His weakness that we may approach Him with confidence.

Lectures on Isaiah (1527–30)
LW 17, 330–31

Thursday

"For my eyes have seen your salvation, which you have prepared in the presence of all peoples, a light for revelation to the Gentiles and for glory to your people Israel." And the child's father and mother were amazed at what was being said about him.   Luke 2:30-33

The evangelist has established here a distinguishing mark: he does not mention Joseph and Mary by name; he calls them father and mother, in order to point out the spiritual meaning. Who, then, are Christ's spiritual father and mother? He himself names his spiritual mother in Mark 3:34-35: "He who does the will of my father, that one is my brother, my sister, and my mother." St. Paul calls himself a father in 1 Corinthians 4:15. Thus the Christian church, that is, all believing persons, is Christ's spiritual mother, and all apostles and teachers of the people, who preach the gospel, are his spiritual father. As often as a person becomes a believer, Christ is born of them. These are the people who marvel over the statements of the prophets, that they apply so nicely and accurately to Christ, speak of him so gloriously, and bear witness to the whole gospel so masterfully. There is no greater joy in this life than to see and experience this in Scripture.

Sermon on "The Gospel for the Sunday after Christmas, Luke 2[:33-40]" (1522)
LW 52, 107

Friday

Jesus said to him, "I am the way, and the truth, and the life. No one comes to the Father except through me."   John 14:6

Whenever you consider the doctrine of justification and wonder how or where or in what condition to find a God who justifies or accepts sinners, then you must know that there is no other God than this Man Jesus Christ. Take hold of Him; cling to Him with all your heart, and spurn all speculation about the Divine Majesty; for whoever investigates the majesty of God will be consumed by His glory. Christ Himself says, "I am the Way . . ." (John 14:6).

You must pay attention only to this Man, who presents Himself to us as the Mediator and says: "Come to Me, all who labor . . ." (Matt. 11:28). When you do this, you will see the love, the goodness, and the sweetness of God. You will see His wisdom, His power, and His majesty sweetened and mitigated to your ability to stand it. And in this lovely picture you will find everything, as Paul says to the Colossians 2: "In Christ are hid all the treasures of wisdom and knowledge"; and "In Him the whole fullness of deity dwells bodily." The world does not see this, because it looks at Him only as a man in His weakness.

That is why Paul makes such a frequent practice of linking Jesus Christ with God the Father, to teach us what is the true Christian religion. It does not begin at the top, as all other religions do; it begins at the bottom. You must run directly to the manger and the mother's womb, embrace this Infant and Virgin's Child in your arms, and look at Him—born, being nursed, growing up, going about in human society, teaching, dying, rising again, ascending above all the heavens, and having authority over all things.

Lectures on Galatians (1535)
LW 26, 29–30

KNOWING GOD

May God, who has led and called you to a knowledge of the truth, strengthen and preserve you to his praise and glory. To him and to his grace I commend you. Amen.

Letters, 213

Monday

"Believe in God, believe also in me."
John 14:1b

Christ wants to say here: "You have heard that you must trust in God. But I want to show you where you will truly find Him, lest your thoughts create an idol bearing the name of God. If you want to believe in God, then believe in Me. If you want to apply your faith and your confidence properly, that it may not be amiss or false, then direct it toward Me, for in Me the entire Godhead dwells perfectly."

Later Christ declares (John 14:6, 9): "I am the Way, the Truth and the Life. He who has seen Me has seen the Father. He who hears Me hears the Father. Therefore if you want to be sure to meet God, take hold of Him in Me and through Me."

Repeatedly in the Gospels Christ declares that He was sent by the Father. He says and does nothing of His own accord, but states that it is the Father's order and command to all the world to believe Christ as God Himself. Thus no one dare adopt another person or means to apprehend God than this one Christ. He assures us that if we rely on Him, we will not encounter an idol, as the others do who resort to other ways to deal with God.

It is certain that those who bypass the Person of Christ never find the true God. Since God is fully in Christ, where He places Himself for us, no effort to deal with God without and apart from Christ on the strength of human thoughts and devotion will be successful.

Whoever would travel the right road and not go astray with his faith, let them begin where God says and where He wants to be found, in this Man—Jesus Christ.

Sermons on the Gospel of St. John (1537–38)
LW 24, 17, 23

Have mercy on me, O God, according to
your steadfast love; according to your
abundant mercy blot out my transgressions.
    Psalm 51:1

Tuesday

David is talking to the God of his fathers—the God who promised. The people of Israel did not have a God who was viewed "absolutely." Human weakness cannot help being crushed by the majesty of the absolute God, as Scripture reminds us over and over. Let no one, therefore, interpret David as speaking with the absolute God.

He is speaking with God as He is dressed and clothed in His Word and promises, so that from the name "God" we cannot exclude Christ, whom God promised to Adam and the other patriarchs. We must take hold of this God, not naked but clothed and revealed in His Word. Otherwise certain despair will crush us.

This distinction must always be made between the Prophets who speak with God and the pagans. Pagans speak with God outside His Word and promises, according to the thoughts of their own hearts. But the Prophets speak with God as He is clothed and revealed in His promises and Word. This God, clothed in such a kind appearance and dressed in His promises—this God we can grasp and look at with joy and trust. The absolute God, on the other hand, is like an iron wall, against which we cannot bump without destroying ourselves. Therefore Satan is busy day and night, making us run to the naked God so that we forget His promises and blessings shown in Christ and think about God and the judgment of God.

But David speaks with the God of his fathers, with the God whose promises he knows and whose mercy and grace he has felt. He could depend on God's promises as he prayed because the promises include Christ.

Commentary on "Psalm 51" (1532)
LW 12, 312–13

Wednesday

For when God made his promise to Abraham, he made a vow to do what he had promised. Hebrews 6:13a (TEV)

Chrysostom says: ". . . by means of these words (the apostle) comforts . . . by showing God's customary way of doing things. . . . It is not His custom to fulfill His promises swiftly but to do so after a long time." Therefore those who want to serve God must learn to know His will and His custom. For who can serve a master whom they do not know?

But to learn to know God in nature the way the philosophers learned to know His power and His essence (Rom. 1:20) is not enough. One must learn to know what His will or what His plan is.

This He shows in His commandments, as Ps. 103:7 states: "He made known His ways to Moses and His will to the Children of Israel." But no one understands His commandments, either, unless illumined anew from above. "For who among mortals will be able to know the counsel of God, or who will be able to think what God's will is?" (Wisd. 9:13). Likewise (1 Cor. 2:11, 10): "The things of God no one knows but the Spirit of God. But God has revealed them to us through His Spirit."

And so we read in Ps. 119 "Teach me," "Instruct me," "Give me understanding." With all these words not only God's essence but especially His will is commended. Therefore those who presume to grasp Holy Scripture and the Law of God with their own intellect and to understand them by their own effort are exceedingly in error. For this is the source of heresies and godless dogmas, since they approach, not as receptive pupils but as bustling teachers.

"Lectures on Hebrews" (1517)
LW 29, 185–86

"I have made known to you everything that I heard from my Father."
John 15:15b

These are beautiful and comforting words. Christ says to us: "If you want to know the Father's will and thought in heaven, you have all the information right here, for I have told you everything." A Christian can arrive at this definite conclusion and say: "God be praised, I know everything that God wants and has at heart. Nothing that serves my salvation is concealed from me."

Christ is not saying that we are to have an answer to every question, but that we have God's whole plan and counsel for us. If you want to be certain what God in heaven thinks of you, you must not seclude yourself, retire into some nook, and brood about it or seek the answer in your works or in your contemplation. Banish all this from your heart. Give ear solely to the words of this Christ, for everything is revealed in Him.

And here He declares: "I was sent to you by My Father that I might shed My blood and die for you. As a token of this you have Baptism and the Sacrament, and I ask you to believe this. Here you have all that I know and have heard from the Father. The Father has no other plan and intention toward you than to save you if you have Christ and faith. From this you see how I love you, and what friendship, glory, joy, consolation, and assurance you have from Me. You cannot attain this anywhere else, either in heaven or on earth."

Sermons on the Gospel of St. John (1537)
LW 24, 257

Friday

But in these last days he has spoken to us by a Son, whom he appointed heir of all things, through whom he also created the worlds.   Hebrews 1:2

The writer describes the same Christ as the Son of Man and the Son of God. For the words "He was appointed the Heir of all things" are properly applicable to Him because of His humanity. But the words "the worlds were made through Him" apply to Him because of His divinity.

One should also note that he mentions the humanity of Christ before he mentions His divinity, in order that he may establish the well-known rule that one learns to know God in faith. For the humanity is that holy ladder of ours, mentioned in Gen. 28:12, by which we ascend to the knowledge of God.

Therefore Christ says: "No one comes to the Father but by Me" (John 14:6). And again: "I am the Door" (John 10:7). He who wants to ascend advantageously to the love and knowledge of God should abandon the human metaphysical rules concerning knowledge of the divinity and apply himself first to the humanity of Christ. For it is exceedingly godless temerity that, where God has humiliated Himself in order to become recognizable, mortals seek for themselves another way by following the counsels of their own natural capacity. For Christ is the image of the invisible God, as it says in Col. 1:15.

"Lectures on Hebrews" (1517)
LW 29, 110–11

EPIPHANY

Almighty eternal God, we heartily pray, grant that we may know and praise your dear Son as did St. Simeon, who took him up in his arms and spiritually knew and confessed him; through the same your Son Jesus Christ our Lord. Amen.

LW 53, 132

Monday

There was also a prophet, Anna. . . . She never left the temple but worshiped there with fasting and prayer night and day. At that moment she came, and began to praise God and to speak about the child to all who were looking for the redemption of Jerusalem.   Luke 2:36-38

This saintly woman was also shown that she was worthy of great honor in that she received the grace to recognize in this poor child the true Savior. Undoubtedly, there were priests present who received similar offerings from Mary and Joseph and yet did not recognize the child and who, perhaps, considered the words of Simeon and Anna as old wives' tales. There must have been a special illumination of the Spirit in her, and she must have been regarded as a great saint in the eyes of God, that he gave her the light in preference to all other people. Notice that there are five persons meeting together: the Christ-child, his mother Mary, Joseph, Simeon, and Anna; yet in that small number various stations of life are represented: man and woman, young and old, virgin and widow, married and unmarried. Thus at a very early age Christ begins to gather to himself all stations which are blessed; he does not care to be alone. Therefore whoever is not found in one of these states, is not in the state of blessedness.

Sermon on "The Gospel for the Sunday after Christmas,
Luke 2[:33-40]" (1522)
LW 52, 140–41

[Anna] began to praise God and to speak about the child to all who were looking for the redemption of Jerusalem.
Luke 2:38b

Tuesday

Furthermore, Anna did not only thank God, but she also spoke of him to all who were awaiting the redemption. Luke does not idly add that Anna spoke of Christ only to those who were waiting for the redemption. Undoubtedly there were not many, and none among the superlearned priests. What could such high, holy, educated people learn from listening to an old, foolish woman? That is undoubtedly the way her words were regarded by these great lords.

Therefore it is received only by the hungry and longing souls who are awaiting redemption, as Luke says here; those who feel their sins, yearn for light and consolation, and who know nothing of any wisdom and righteousness of their own. Faith and knowledge of Christ cannot remain silent. Faith breaks forth and testifies in order to help others and to share its light, as Psalm 116:10 says: "I have believed, and so I also speak." Faith is much too kind and good to keep such treasure for itself alone.

Sermon on "The Gospel for the Sunday after Christmas,
Luke 2[:33-40]" (1522)
LW 52, 142–43

Epiphany

Wednesday

They shall bring gold and frankincense, and shall proclaim the praise of the LORD. . . . [from] Tarshish . . . their silver and gold with them, for the name of the LORD your God. . .   Isaiah 60:6b, 9b

Some apply this to the Magi (Matt. 2:11). I am well satisfied with that application. The proper meaning is that these people revere God and the Gospel with the same zeal and wealth with which they do homage to other kings. Now that the Gospel has arisen, they do homage to the Gospel with every kind of wealth. This happens in our case when we receive the glory of the Lord and for its sake are ready to give up body and life, our money, all things.

So here some have interpreted the gold and silver as referring to wisdom and eloquence. I let the gold and silver stand for the resources. People who have been drawn into the church and to a love of the neighbor by faithfulness in faith and true love share what they have with a trusting heart and diligent hand. If I have won someone's heart, I will soon have his purse too. To the glory of God the faithful return nothing, but freely bestow themselves and their goods on the poor and in simplicity show themselves grateful toward the mercy of God. Other religions seek their own name and advantage and glory and wealth. But here Christians, for the free forgiveness of sins and for the gifts of the Holy Spirit which they have received, seek not their own but the things that are God's.

Lectures on Isaiah (1527–30)
LW 17, 314–15, 317

On entering the house, they saw the child
with Mary his mother; and they knelt
down and paid him homage.
Matthew 2:11a

Thursday

Thus the Magi teach us true faith. After they had heard the sermon and the word of the prophet they were neither slothful nor slow to believe. Note the obstructions and obstacles they faced: first, they were off the mark; they came to Jerusalem the capital, and did not find him; and in the meantime the star disappeared. Would we not expect that their thoughts, if guided by human reason, would have been as follows: "Alas, in vain we travelled so far; the star deceived us, it was a phantom. If a king had been born, we would easily have found him in the capital city, lying in the royal palace. But upon our arrival, we find no one who knows of him. Ah, it must all be a mistake. Besides, the news frightens them; his own people do not like hearing it. They show us the way out of the royal city and direct us to a tiny village. Who knows what we will find there!"

When the magi arrive at a poor hut and find there a poor young woman with a poor little child, they meet once again with appearances so utterly out of keeping with a king, that even their domestic servant is more honorable and more noble. But they do not allow all this to make them waver, but with a great, strong, and full faith they dismiss from their eyes and senses whatever human nature in its vanity might question and undermine, and follow the word of the prophet and the witness of the star in all purity of heart, take him to be a king, fall down on their knees, worship him, and give him gifts.

Sermon on "The Gospel for the Festival of the Epiphany,
Matthew 2[:1-12]" (1522)
LW 52, 195, 197

Friday

Wise men from the East came to Jerusalem, asking, "Where is the child who has been born king of the Jews? For we observed his star at its rising, and have come to pay him homage."
Matthew 2:1-2

[At times, Luther still used the traditional method of interpreting Scripture by emphasizing the "spiritual meaning," using persons, things, and events as pointers to life with Christ. Thus, after commenting on the direct meaning of the story of the wise men, Luther gives what he calls the "spiritual meaning" from which the following is an excerpt.]

What is the star? It is none other than the new light, preaching and the gospel, oral and public preaching. Christ has two witnesses to his birth and his realm. The one is Scripture, the word comprehended in the letters of the alphabet. The other is the voice or the words proclaimed by mouth.

Let it suffice for the present that this star signifies oral preaching and the bright revelation of Christ, which shows him as hidden and promised in Scripture. Therefore whoever sees the star will assuredly recognize the King of the Jews, the newborn Christ. For the gospel teaches nothing but Christ, and therefore Scripture contains nothing but Christ. Whoever fails to recognize Christ may hear the gospel or he may indeed carry the book in his hand, but he lacks understanding, for to have the gospel without understanding, is to have no gospel at all. And to possess Scripture without knowing Christ, is to have no Scripture, which is nothing else than to let this star shine, and to fail to see it.

Sermon on "The Gospel for the Festival of the Epiphany, Matthew 2[:1-12]" (1522)
LW 52, 205, 207

THE MISSION OF CHRIST

You, Lord Jesus, are my righteousness, but I am your sin. You have taken upon yourself what is mine and have given to me what is yours. You have taken upon yourself what you were not and have given to me what I was not. Amen.

Letters, 110

The Mission of Christ

Monday

"The Son of Man came not to be served but to serve, and to give his life as a ransom for many." Matthew 20:28

May you ever cherish and treasure this thought. Christ is made a servant to sin, yea, a bearer of sin, and the lowliest and most despised person. He destroys all sin by Himself and says: "I came not to be served but to serve" (Matt. 20:28). There is no greater bondage than that of sin; and there is no greater service than that displayed by the Son of God, who becomes the servant of all, no matter how poor, wretched, or despised they may be, and bears their sins.

It would be spectacular and amazing, prompting all the world to open ears and eyes, mouth and nose in uncomprehending wonderment, if some king's son were to appear in a beggar's home to nurse him in his illness, wash off his filth, and do everything else the beggar would have to do. Would this not be profound humility? Any spectator or any beneficiary of this honor would feel impelled to admit that he had seen or experienced something unusual and extraordinary, something magnificent.

And yet the love of the Son of God for us is of such magnitude that the greater the filth and stench of our sins, the more He befriends us, the more He cleanses us, relieving us of all our misery and of the burden of all our sins and placing them upon His own back.

Whenever the devil declares: "You are a sinner!" Christ interposes: "I will reverse the order; I will be a sinner, and you are to go scotfree." Who can thank our God enough for this mercy?

Sermons on the Gospel of St. John (1537–40)
LW 22, 166–67

The Mission of Christ

"Yet even if I do judge, my judgment is valid; for it is not I alone who judge, but I and the Father who sent me."
John 8:16

Tuesday

To be sure, Christ's primary mission is not to judge but to help. This is His real office, and this we must bear in mind. In John 3:17 Christ said: "For God sent the Son into the world, not to condemn the world, but that the world might be saved through Him." This is the chief function of Christ, and to this end He came into the world. But if some will not accept this or submit to Him who would help, then is it Christ's fault that they who reject life are given over to death?

In Genesis 22:18 it is written of Christ: "In your Seed shall all the nations of the earth be blessed." This is to be His title and His office, namely, to bless, to help, to counsel. Here we find the sweet word "bless," help. He is to be a comforting Preacher, a friendly Man and Helper, who will spare no effort and do nothing but teach and work, help and bless. With Him is pure help and consolation. Yet these same words include condemnation, judgment, and sentence. Wherever a blessing is rejected, there a curse follows. Those who will not have help and comfort must take damnation. Those who will not be well must remain sick. Those who will not go to heaven must go to hell. Although it is not part of Christ's office to consign to hell, to curse, or to condemn, but to help and rescue, it is equally true that those who scorn this help must remain in hell.

Sermons on the Gospel of St. John (1530–32)
LW 23, 338–39

Wednesday

To whom then will you compare me, or who is my equal? says the Holy One.
Isaiah 40:25

God bids us lift up our head. He sets forth His Word and with it gives Himself to us, so that all things are ours and we, on the other hand, may cast our weakness off on Christ. If I am a sinner, Christ is righteous; if I am poor, Christ is rich; if I am foolish, Christ is wise; if I am a captive, Christ is present to set me free; if I am forsaken, Christ takes me to Himself; if I am cast down, Christ consoles me; if I am weary, Christ refreshes me. Finally, He pours Himself out for me altogether. Should not these things console me, since they cannot be compared with anything for value?

Lectures on Isaiah (1527–30)
LW 17, 28

The Mission of Christ

Here is my servant, whom I uphold, my $\quad$ **Thursday**
chosen, in whom my soul delights; . . .
Isaiah 42:1a

These are words of demonstration, as if he were pointing to something worth seeing. . . . "If you want to know and be wise, look to this Christ, the Doctor and the One in charge and up and doing. Him I have put in charge. Keep your eye on Him, observe what He does, says, and teaches, because He is My Servant." This was not written for Christ's sake but for ours, so that we may be sure about His work and teaching and may have certainty about the emptiness of our idolatry. Nobody understands these things unless he believes. You must believe that Christ is a servant as stated in this passage. Here we have the most reliable voice, and this teaching is for us. But we see from experience that nothing is more absurd to the wisdom of the flesh than Christ, the Servant, and His Word. All are offended because of Him. All of us want to be God's servants while we please ourselves.

But for Christ, here, in the time of his earthly life, He will be Servant. After death He will be Lord. In His life He will be the most prudent Servant.

Lectures on Isaiah (1527–30)
LW 17, 60–61, 216

Friday

For Jesus is the one who leads them to salvation.   Hebrews 2:10 (TEV)

God the Father made Christ to be the Sign and Idea in order that those who adhere to Him by faith might be transformed into the same image (2 Cor. 3:18) and thus be drawn away from the images of the world. Therefore Isaiah says: "The Lord will raise an Ensign for the nations, and will assemble the outcasts of Israel," and "The Root of Jesse which stands as an Ensign to the peoples; Him shall the nations seek" (Isaiah 11:12, 10).

This gathering together of the children of God is similar to what happens when the government arranges a spectacle to which the citizens flock. They leave their work and their homes and fix their attention on it alone. Thus through the Gospel as through a spectacle exhibited to the whole world (cf. 2 Cor. 4:9) Christ attracts all people by the knowledge and contemplation of Himself and draws them away from the things to which they have clung in the world.

In this way Christ is the Cause and Leader of salvation, for He draws and leads His children to glory through Him. One would commonly say that Christ is the Instrument and the Means by which God leads His children. For God does not compel believers to salvation by force and fear, but by this pleasing spectacle of His mercy and love He moves and draws through love all those whom He will save.

"Lectures on Hebrews" (1517–18)
LW 29, 132

ADAM AND EVE

Lord God, heavenly Father, who has no pleasure in the death of poor sinners and would not willingly let them perish, but desires that they should return from their ways and live: We heartily ask you graciously to avert the well-deserved punishment of our sins and tenderly to grant us your mercy for our future amendment; for the sake of Jesus Christ our Lord. Amen.

LW 53, 140

Adam and Eve

Monday

"And let them have dominion over the fish of the sea, and over the birds of the air, and over the cattle, and over all the wild animals of the earth, and over every creeping thing that creeps upon the earth."
Genesis 1:26

Here the rule is assigned to the most beautiful creature[s], who know God and are the image of God, in whom the similitude of the divine nature shines forth through their enlightened reason, through their justice and wisdom. Adam and Eve become the rulers of the earth, the sea, and the air. Who can conceive of that part, as it were, of the divine nature, that Adam and Eve had insight into all the dispositions of all animals, into their characters and all their powers?

Eve had these mental gifts in the same degree as Adam, as Eve's utterance shows when she answered the serpent concerning the tree in the middle of Paradise. There it becomes clear enough that she knew to what end she had been created and pointed to the source from which she had this knowledge; for she said (Gen. 3:3): "The Lord said." Thus she not only heard this from Adam, but her very nature was pure and full of knowledge of God to such a degree that by herself she knew the Word of God and understood it.

It is a good thing to know these facts and to ponder them, so that we may have a longing for that coming Day when that which we lost in Paradise through sin will be restored to us.

Lectures on Genesis (1535–36)
LW 1, 66–67

Adam and Eve

Out of the ground the LORD God made to grow every tree that is pleasant to the sight and good for food, the tree of life also in the midst of the garden and the tree of the knowledge of good and evil.
Genesis 2:9

Surrounded as Adam was by the goodness of the Creator, if he had remained in the state of innocence, he would have acknowledged God as his Creator and would have governed the beasts according to His will without any inconvenience, in fact, with extreme joy. For all things were such that they could not harm humans but could delight them in the highest degree.

And so when Adam had been created in such a way that he was, as it were, intoxicated with rejoicing toward God and was delighted also with all the other creatures, there is now created a new tree for the distinguishing of good and evil, so that Adam might have a definite way to express his worship and reverence toward God. After everything had been entrusted to him to make use of it according to his will, whether he wished to do so for necessity or for pleasure, God finally demands from Adam that at this tree of the knowledge of good and evil he demonstrate his reverence and obedience toward God and that he maintain this practice, as it were, of worshiping God by not eating anything from it.

Lectures on Genesis (1535–36)
LW 1, 93–94

Adam and Eve

Wednesday

Lord, you have been our dwelling place in all generations.   Psalm 90:1

Why does he add the phrase "from generation to generation"? Surely in order to signify that the one church endures from the beginning of the creation of man to the end of the world. This is what he says: "From the day that a generation of human beings or time began Thou art our Dwelling Place," as though he were telling us: "The church has always existed; there has always been a people of God from the time of the first person Adam to the very latest infant born."

Thus somewhere in his writings Anselm draws this surprising but nevertheless good and true conclusion: Adam and Eve were Christians and justified sinners, and it was an inescapable necessity that immediately after the Fall they returned by faith to the true way, so that there might not be a time when the church did not exist. Immediately after their fall into sin Adam and Eve were seized with contrition and filled with fear (Gen. 3:8-10).

Since, however, God afterwards gave the promise of the woman's Seed (Gen. 3:15), Adam and Eve were in reality justified by faith in Christ. Indeed, they fled from God because of their fear of God's wrath and future punishment. But God sought them of His own free will and reinstated them. This was the first church. It was begotten through the Word and justified by faith in Christ.

For the church cannot but be and continue, even as Moses shows here when he says that God is the Dwelling Place of humanity from generation to generation.

Commentary on "Psalm 90" (1534–35)
LW 13, 88, 90–91

Adam and Eve

"I will put enmity between you and the woman, and between your offspring and hers."   *Genesis 3:15*

Thursday

These words deal specifically with the judgment of Satan. Here we find sound comfort, for these words are not spoken by God for the devil's sake. They are spoken for the sake of Adam and Eve, that hearing this judgment, they may be comforted, realizing that God is the enemy of that being which inflicted so severe a wound on humanity.

Here grace and mercy begin to shine forth from the midst of the wrath which sin and disobedience aroused. Here, in the midst of most serious threats, the Father reveals His heart. This is not a father who is so angry that he would turn out his son because of his sin, but one who points to a deliverance. Indeed, this father promises victory against the enemy that deceived and conquered human nature.

Adam and Eve do not hear themselves cursed like the serpent. No, they hear themselves drawn up, as it were, in the battle line against their conquered enemy, with the hope of help from the Son of God, the Seed [offspring] of the woman. Forgiveness of sins and full reception into grace are here pointed out to Adam and Eve.

Their consolation against sin and despair was their hope for this crushing of Satan by the Seed. It would be brought about in the future through Christ. And through the hope based on this promise, Adam and Eve will also rise up to eternal life on the Last Day.

Lectures on Genesis (1535–36)
LW 1, 188–91

Adam and Eve

Friday

The man named his wife Eve, because she was the mother of all living.
Genesis 3:20

The name which Adam gives his wife is very pleasing and delightful. For what is more precious, better, or more delightful than life? This is the reason he gave: "Because she is the mother of all living." It is clear from this passage that after Adam had received the Holy Spirit, he had become marvelously enlightened. He believed and understood the saying concerning the woman's Seed who would crush the head of the serpent.

He gave an outward indication of this faith by means of his wife's name. By this designation of his wife he gave support to the hope in the future Seed. He strengthened his own faith and comforted himself with the thought that he believed in life even when all nature had already been made subject to death.

If Adam had not been aware of the future life, he would not have been able to cheer his heart, nor would he have assigned so pleasing a name to his wife. But here he gives clear indication that the Holy Spirit had cheered his heart through his trust in the forgiveness of sins by the Seed of Eve. He calls her Eve to remind himself of the promise through which he himself also received new life, and to pass on the hope of eternal life to his descendants.

Lectures on Genesis (1535–36)
LW 1, 219–20

NOAH

Lord God Almighty, who does not disdain the sighs of the forlorn or scorn the longing of troubled hearts: Behold our prayer which we bring before you in our need and graciously hear us, so that all which strives against us of both the devil and humanity may come to nought and be scattered by your good counsel, to the end that unhurt by all temptation we may thank you in your church and praise you at all times; through Jesus your Son our Lord. Amen.

LW 53, 140

Monday

Noah was a righteous man, blameless in his generation; Noah walked with God.
Genesis 6:9b

Earlier, in speaking of the story of Enoch [Genesis 5:21-24], we gave the meaning of "to walk with God," namely, to carry on the business of God in public. To be righteous and perfect is evidence of personal excellence; but to walk with God is something public, namely, to carry on God's business before the world, to occupy oneself with His Word, and to teach His worship. Noah was not only righteous and holy so far as his own person was concerned, but he was also a confessor. He informed others of the promises and threats of God, and in that most wicked and depraved age he carried out and suffered everything that is the obligation of a person in a public position.

Lectures on Genesis (ca. 1536)
LW 2, 56

And God said to Noah, "I have determined to make an end of all flesh, for the earth is filled with violence because of them."
Genesis 6:13

Tuesday

What is the reason for this great wrath? Certainly, as the text states here, it is to be found in the fact that the earth is filled with violence. An amazing reason! The text says nothing about the First Table of the Law. It stresses only the Second Table, as though God intended to say: "About Myself I shall say nothing. I shall not say that they hate, blaspheme, and persecute My name and Word. But how disgracefully they live among themselves! Neither the household nor the state is properly managed; everything is done with violence, nothing with reason and law. Therefore I shall destroy both humankind and the earth."

It is the abundance of His compassion and love that causes God to complain more about the wrongs with which His members are oppressed than about those that are inflicted on Him. We see that He is silent about the latter in this passage when He threatens destruction not only for humankind but also for the earth.

Lectures on Genesis (ca. 1536)
LW 2, 65

Wednesday

Then the Lord said to Noah, "Go into the ark, you and all your household, for I have seen that you alone are righteous before me in this generation. Take with you seven pairs of all clean animals, the male and its mate; and a pair of the animals that are not clean, the male and its mate; and seven pairs of the birds of the air also, male and female, to keep their kind alive on the face of all the earth." Genesis 7:1-3

It is obvious that God enjoys talking to Noah. It is not enough for Him to have given him orders once about what he should do, but He repeats the same orders in the same words. Reason considers this wordiness absurd, but to a heart battling desperation nothing that gives instruction about God's will can seem to be enough or too much. God sees this attitude of the heart in its trial. He repeats the same words in close succession in order that Noah, as a result of that conversation and wordiness, may realize that he is not only not forsaken even though the entire world may have forsaken him but has a friendly and kindly disposed God, who loves him so much that it seems He cannot converse enough with this pious man. This is the reason why the same statements are repeated in this passage.

Lectures on Genesis (ca. 1536)
LW 2, 88

*But God remembered Noah and all the
wild animals and all the domestic animals
that were with him in the ark.
Genesis 8:1a*

Thursday

It is not idle chatter when the Holy Spirit says that God remembered Noah. It indicates that from the day when Noah entered the ark nothing was said to him, nothing was revealed to him, and he saw no ray of grace shining. He clung only to the promise he had received.

Meanwhile the waters and the waves were raging as though God had surely forgotten him. His children, the cattle and the other animals experienced the same peril throughout the entire hundred and fifty days in the ark. Even though the holy seed overcame these perils, through the rich measure of the Spirit, it did not overcome them without tears and great fear.

It was no joke or laughing matter for them to live shut up in the ark for so long, to see the endless masses of rain, to be tossed about by the waves, and to drift. In these circumstances there was the feeling that God had forgotten them. All their circumstances compelled them to debate whether God was favorably inclined and wanted to remember them. Therefore, although they overcame these hardships, they did not overcome them without awful affliction.

Let us, then, remember that this story sets before us an example of faith, perseverance, and patience, in order that those who have the divine promise may not only learn to believe it but may also realize that they need perseverance. In the New Testament Christ calls on us to persevere when He says: "[The one] who endures to the end will be saved" (Matt. 24:13).

Lectures on Genesis (ca. 1536)
LW 2, 103–5

Noah

Friday

God said, "This is the sign of the covenant that I make between me and you and every living creature that is with you, for all future generations: I have set my bow in the clouds, and it shall be a sign of the covenant between me and the earth."

Genesis 9:12-13

Careful note must be taken of the phrase "for all future generations," for it includes not only the human beings of that time and the animals of that time but all their offspring until the end of the world. Furthermore, this passage also teaches us how God often links His promise with a sign.

Noah and his people were in great need of such comfort. One who has been humbled by God is unable to forget the hurt and pain. It is for this reason that God shows Himself benevolent in such a variety of ways and takes such extraordinary delight in pouring forth compassion.

This comfort is expressed in many eloquent words and emphasized by the sign of the bow to meet the need of these wretched people who had been watching the immeasurable wrath of God rage for an entire year. They could not be talked out of their fear and terror by a word or two. A great abundance of words was needed to drive back their tears and to soften their grief. Even though they were saints, they were still flesh, just as we are.

When the same matter is repeated so many times (Genesis 9:11-16), this is an indication of God's extraordinary affection for humankind. He is trying to persuade them not to fear such a punishment in the future but to hope for blessing and for the utmost forbearance.

Lectures on Genesis (ca. 1536)
LW 2, 144–45

ABRAHAM

Be a merciful Father and do not take us to task, but grant us your grace that your name may be hallowed in us. Let us not think, say, do, have, or undertake anything unless it redounds to your honor and glory. Grant that we may enhance your name and honor above everything else and that we not seek our own vainglory nor further our own name. Grant that we may love and fear and honor you as children do their father. Amen.

LW 42, 78

Abraham

Monday

I will instruct you and teach you the way you should go; I will counsel you with my eye upon you.   Psalm 32:8

[It is as if God were saying:] This is where I want you to be. You ask that I deliver you. Then do not be uneasy about it, do not teach Me, and do not teach yourself; surrender yourself to Me. I am competent to be your Master. I will lead you in a way that is pleasing to Me. You think it wrong if things do not go as you feel they should. But your thinking harms you and hinders Me. Things must go, not according to your understanding but above your understanding. Submerge yourself in a lack of understanding, and I will give you My understanding. Lack of understanding is real understanding; not knowing where you are going is really knowing where you are going. My understanding makes you without understanding.

Thus Abraham went out from his homeland and did not know where he was going. He yielded to My knowledge and abandoned his own knowledge. By the right way he reached the right goal.

Behold, that is the way of the cross. You cannot find it, but I must lead you like a blind person. Therefore not you, not a human being, not a creature, but I, through My Spirit and the Word, will teach you the way you must go. You must not follow the work which you choose, not the suffering which you devise, but that which comes to you against your choice, thoughts, and desires. There I call; there you must be a pupil; there it is the time; there your Master has come; there you must not be a horse or an irrational animal. If you follow Me and forsake yourself, behold, then "I will counsel you with My eye upon you."

Commentary on "The Seven Penitential Psalms" (1525)
LW 14, 152

There was strife between the herders of Abram's livestock and the herders of Lot's livestock. . . . Then Abram said to Lot, "Let there be no strife."
Genesis 13:7-8a

Tuesday

It was no minor matter that in the midst of strange nations Abram was compelled to separate from a very faithful companion and dear nephew. A faithful friend is a great boon and a precious treasure in any situation of life. He can give aid and comfort in facing common dangers and also during spiritual trials. Even if one's heart is well grounded by the Holy Spirit, it is a great advantage to have a brother with whom one can talk about religion and from whom one can hear words of comfort.

To keep us from supposing that this parting of relatives occurred as the result of insignificant events, the Scripture gives weighty reasons why Abram and Lot separated. Nothing sadder could happen to Abram, but he yields to necessity in order to avoid even greater unpleasantness.

But let us take note of the law of love and of unity. Abram was Lot's uncle; he was older; he had greater prestige because of the promise. In addition, he was a priest and prophet of the Lord. And yet, disregarding all this, he yields his right and puts himself on the same level with his nephew. "If you take the left hand," Abram says to Lot, "then I will go to the right; or if you take the right hand, then I will go to the left." He gives Lot the choice. Is this not what Christ commands in John 13:15ff., that he who is the greater should be as the lesser and as the servant of the others?

Lectures on Genesis (ca. 1536)
LW 2, 335–37

Abraham

Wednesday

He brought him outside and said, "Look toward heaven and count the stars, if you are able to count them." Then he said to him, "So shall your descendants be."
Genesis 15:5

The fact that Abraham is commanded to look at the stars is proof that this vision occurred at night, at a time when Abraham was sighing and lamenting. It is characteristic of sublime trials to occupy hearts when they are alone. For this reason there is frequent mention in the Holy Scripture of praying at night and in solitude. Affliction is the teacher of such praying.

Thus because Abraham was occupied with these sad thoughts, he was unable to sleep. Therefore he got up and prayed; but while he is praying and feeling such great agitation within himself, God appears to him and converses with him in a friendly manner, so that Abraham, who is awake, is completely enraptured.

The trial which tormented this saintly man was not a light one. Therefore God's message to Abraham is profuse and His encouragement lavish, even adding a sign. Abraham is led out. He is told to look toward heaven and to count the stars. And innumerable descendants are promised him by God who does not indulge in empty talk.

God speaks with Abraham in a manner that is no different from the way a friend speaks with a close acquaintance. It is God's practice to do so, and this is His nature.

After He has properly afflicted His own, He shows Himself most benevolent and pours Himself out completely.

Lectures on Genesis (1538)
LW 3, 17–18

And [Abram] believed the Lord; and the   # Thursday
Lord reckoned it to him as righteousness.
Genesis 15:6

Faith had previously been mentioned in other Genesis passages—for example, the passage about the Seed of the woman, the command to build the ark, the threat of the Flood, and the command to Abraham to leave his country. But these passages merely demand faith; they do not praise or recommend it. They do not commend faith as the verse before us does. Therefore this is one of the foremost passages of all Scripture.

If you should ask whether Abraham was righteous before this time, my answer is: He was righteous because he believed God. But here the Holy Spirit wanted to attest this expressly since the promise [Gen. 15:5] deals with a spiritual Seed. He did so in order that you might conclude on the basis of a correct inference that those who accept this Seed, or those who believe in Christ, are righteous.

Abraham's faith was extraordinary, since he left his country when commanded to do so and became an exile; but we are not all commanded to do the same thing. Therefore in that connection Moses does not add: "Abraham believed God, and this was reckoned to him as righteousness." But in the passage before us he makes this addition when he is speaking about the heavenly Seed. He does so in order to comfort the church of all times. [Romans 4:23-24; 15:4]. He is saying that those who, with Abraham, believe this promise are truly righteous.

Lectures on Genesis (1538)
LW 3, 19–20

Abraham

Friday

Then Abraham fell on his face and laughed, and said to himself, "Can a child be born to a man who is a hundred years old? Can Sarah, who is ninety years old, bear a child?"   Genesis 17:17

Even though Abraham had no doubts about the promise, yet so far he was mistaken with respect to the person. For he thought that Sarah would not bear a child and that the promise would be diverted to Ishmael. But here a perfect circle is closed, so to speak, and Abraham sees that a true heir will be born to him from Sarah. Consequently, he is full of joy. Exulting and triumphing in the most beautiful and perfect faith, he falls to the ground and laughs. Full of wonderment, he says: "Shall a son be born to me, a man one hundred years old, and from Sarah at that?"

Thus Abraham, full of joy, laughs as he gives thanks to God for His so unexpected kindness. For what else could he do than marvel at this and rejoice over it?

When we read such accounts, we should justly be ashamed that a like fervor of the spirit is not felt in our hearts. Although we have the Word of God in such richness, our hearts are nevertheless harder than an anvil and, like rocky soil, keep the root of the Word without sap and fruit, while the saintly patriarchs marveled at this inexpressible benevolence of God to the point of being overcome.

Let us ask God to give us a joyful heart for such joyful promises that we, too, may exult and be glad with saintly Abraham because we are the people of God.

Lectures on Genesis (1538)
LW 3, 153–55

JOSEPH

O Father, with your divine Word comfort me, a poor and miserable wretch. I cannot bear your hand, and yet I know that it works to my damnation if I do not bear it. Therefore, strengthen me, my Father, lest I despair. Amen.

LW 42, 51

Joseph

Monday

So Joseph went after his brothers, and found them at Dothan. They saw him from a distance, and before he came near to them, they conspired to kill him.

Genesis 37:17b-18

Joseph sets out for his brothers with a ready heart. But he does not know what great danger is threatening him and how very close to him destruction is. For he is not warned by anyone, and God Himself permits him to fall into the hands of his cruel brothers. He pretends not to notice those things which the brothers were planning openly. All the angels and God Himself are silent!

But it is great and noteworthy consolation for us that we see God governing the saintly patriarchs exactly as He governs us. For He does not lead them only by miracles and lofty exercises of the Spirit exceeding the common grasp of godly men, but He confronts them also with the daily dangers, misfortunes, and accidents that can befall any one of us. The excellent Joseph, a model of innocence, is 17, has the Holy Spirit, and is full of the grace of God and His goodwill. He has also lived a very saintly life in the church of his father Jacob, but he is overwhelmed by a wretched misfortune, not unusual for us, perhaps, but quite unworthy of such a saintly man.

Therefore it is an example that belongs to our consolation. For if such experience befell the patriarchs, who were full of the Holy Spirit, why are we surprised or why do we murmur when we suffer similar trials? Let us therefore mutually exhort one another to endurance by the examples of these men, who were like us in the bearing of the cross.

Lectures on Genesis (1542–44)
LW 6, 350–51

Joseph

But the Lord was with Joseph and showed him steadfast love; he gave him favor in the sight of the chief jailer.
Genesis 39:21

Tuesday

Let us learn the rule and order which God is wont to employ in governing His saints. For I, too, have often attempted to prescribe to God definite methods He should use in the administration of the church or of other matters. "Ah, Lord," I have said, "I would like this to be done in this order, with this result!" But God would do the very opposite of what I had sought.

Then the thought would come to me: "Nevertheless, my plan is not disadvantageous to the glory of God. It will contribute very much toward the hallowing of your name, the gathering and increasing of your kingdom, and the propagation of the knowledge of your Word. It is a very fine plan and excellently thought out." But the Lord undoubtedly laughed at this wisdom and said: "Come now, I know that you are a wise and learned man; but it has never been My custom for Peter, Dr. Martin, or anyone else to teach, direct, govern, and lead Me. I am not a passive God. No, I am an active God who is accustomed to doing the leading, ruling, and directing."

Therefore, let us learn from the example of Joseph concerning the way God governs His saints. Here one sees how God carved out and formed this dearly beloved and most precious gem through great trials that were not Joseph's plans but God's plans. These things are set before the church of God and the consciences of the godly to the end that they may learn to understand the nature of the counsels and works of God.

Lectures on Genesis (1544)
LW 7, 103–4

Joseph

Wednesday

The chief jailer paid no heed to anything that was in Joseph's care, because the LORD was with him; and whatever he did, the LORD made it prosper.
Genesis 39:23

If Joseph had said: "Lord God, allow me to live with my father in Hebron," or if he had murmured against God because of the unjust accusation and captivity, and God had satisfied his wishes not to be consigned to slavery or hurled into bonds, then, according to the wisdom of his own reason, which finds it difficult to render this obedience to God, he would never have been raised to such a position of honor. But since he was full of the Holy Spirit, he submitted patiently to the Lord's will until at length he was exalted not only for his own consolation and glory but also for the temporal and spiritual welfare of Egypt. For he saw God's back and waited until God should reveal and show forth His salvation, which is far richer and far more magnificent than he would ever have had the courage to pray or hope for.

Joseph believes in the Lord, whom he does not see. He hopes to have His grace, which he does not perceive. He feels that everything unfavorable is being put in his way. Nevertheless, he receives what he has believed and hoped for.

Up to now he has walked like a blind man in the thickest darkness. He has seen neither God nor his father nor anything else than death and destruction. But he has clung to the Word which he had heard from his father: "I am the Lord your God, and the God of your fathers." This Word has been his life, and from this life he will later be raised to immeasurable glory and honor.

Lectures on Genesis (1544)
LW 7, 105–6

Joseph

They said to him, "We have had dreams, and there is no one to interpret them." And Joseph said to them, "Do not interpretations belong to God? Please tell them to me." . . . Then Joseph said to him, "This is its interpretation." Genesis 40:8, 12a

A prayer undoubtedly preceded these words, for these things were not done as quickly as they are described in brief by Moses. After Joseph had heard the account of the dream, he withdrew to some solitary place and prayed on bended knees. For the saints do nothing without blessing and prayer. They do not rush suddenly into their business but approach it with fear. And because they hope in the Lord, they call upon Him. Even if external gestures are not always employed, they nevertheless pray from the heart, with sobbing and sighs.

Lectures on Genesis (1544)
LW 7, 112

Joseph

Friday

And Pharaoh said to Joseph, "See, I have set you over all the land of Egypt." Removing his signet ring from his hand, Pharaoh put it on Joseph's hand; he arrayed him in garments of fine linen, and put a gold chain around his neck.
Genesis 41:41-42

It is not in our nature to be victorious over oneself when things go well. Yet amid such great honors and good fortune, when the whole world is now smiling on him, paying attention to him, and honoring him, Joseph rules over himself. He is not proud and boastful but remembers God and the condition from which he had emerged to this pinnacle of fortune and rank.

He remembers that he is the son of a shepherd; he remembers his exile, bondage, and imprisonment; he remembers the Word of God, which teaches us that we are conceived and born in sin. Therefore he retains the fear of God and modesty, just as he did when he was in prison and in servitude. To be sure, he is more cheerful, and he thanks God for his liberation; but he does so reverently and in the fear of God. Later we shall see him being agreeable to his brothers in the friendliest manner.

In Joseph, then, you have an outstanding and memorable example of moderation after such great exaltation. For although much was added to his external dignity and splendor, his humility seems to have been increased together with his dignity. Therefore he heeds in an excellent manner the warning of Sirach: "The greater you are, the more you must humble yourself" (Ecclus. 3:18).

Lectures on Genesis (1544)
LW 7, 178–79, 183

MOSES

Lord God, heavenly Father, you know that because of our human weakness we are not able to stand fast in so many and great dangers. Grant us strength both in body and soul, that by your help we may overcome whatever troubles us because of our sins; for the sake of Jesus Christ our Lord. Amen.

LW 53, 141

Monday

When the LORD saw that [Moses] had turned aside to see, God called to him out of the bush, "Moses! Moses!" And he said, "Here I am."   Exodus 3:4

In his first book [Genesis] Moses teaches how all creatures were created, and (as the chief cause for his writing) whence sin and death came, namely by Adam's fall, through the devil's wickedness. But immediately thereafter, before the coming of the law of Moses, he teaches whence help is to come for the driving out of sin and death, namely, not by the law or humanity's own works (since there was no law as yet), but by "the seed of the woman," Christ, promised to Adam and Abraham, in order that throughout the Scriptures from the beginning faith may be praised above all works and laws and merits. Genesis, therefore, is made up almost entirely of illustrations of faith and unbelief, and of the fruits that faith and unbelief bear. It is an exceedingly evangelical book.

Afterward, in the second book [Exodus], when the world was now full and sunk in blindness so that men and women scarcely knew any longer what sin was or where death came from, God brings Moses forward with the law and selects a special people, in order to enlighten the world again through them, and by the law to reveal sin anew.

Thus Moses, as a perfect lawgiver, fulfilled all the duties of his office. He not only gave the law, but was there when men and women were to fulfil it. When things went wrong, he explained the law and re-established it. Yet his explanations really contain nothing else than faith toward God and love toward one's neighbor, for all God's laws come to that.

"Prefaces to the Old Testament" (1545)
LW 35, 237–39

He humbled you by letting you hunger, then by feeding you with manna ... in order to make you understand that one does not live by bread alone.
Deuteronomy 8:3

Tuesday

To understand these and similar wonderful and faithful promises of God is truly to understand the promise of the First Commandment, in which He says: "I am the Lord your God."

"Yours, yours," He says, "who will show and display Myself to you as God and will not forsake you if only you believe this."

This is what Moses treats in this chapter as in the midst of abundance he sets up and presents the example of manna which was given in the midst of want, in order to call them back from the belly to the Word. Therefore he also repeats at the conclusion: "He brought streams forth for you from hard rock and fed you with manna in the desert ..." For what would you less expect from a rock than water and drink? What less in the desert than bread and food? Why did He not give water from some green tree or cloud of the sky? Why not food from branches or roots or herbs?

He did this that the immeasurable care of God for us might be praised. He is willing and able to turn a rock into your drink, a desert into your food, nakedness into beautiful clothing, poverty into wealth, death into life, shame into glory, evil into good, enemies into friends. See, therefore, how fittingly and aptly Moses uses this miracle of God to explain the meaning of the First Commandment.

Lectures on Deuteronomy (1523–25)
LW 9, 94–96

Moses

Wednesday

The L*ord your God will raise up for you
a prophet like me from among your own
people; you shall heed such a prophet.*
Deuteronomy 18:15

This is the chief passage in this whole book and a clearly expressed prophecy of Christ as the new Teacher. Appropriately, Moses places it here at the end, after he has finished his discourses concerning the priesthood, the kingdom, the government, and the whole worship of God. It is his purpose to show that in the future there will be another priesthood, another kingdom, another worship of God, and another word, by which all of Moses will be set aside. Here Moses clearly describes his own end, and he yields his mastery to the Prophet who is to come. When Moses says: "Heed Him who will be raised up like me," he teaches plainly that his own word is different from the Word of that Prophet.

But there cannot be another word beyond the word of Moses, unless it is the Gospel, since everything that belongs to the teaching of the Law has been transmitted most perfectly and amply by Moses. For what could be added to the Decalog, to say nothing of the rest? What loftier thing can be taught than to believe, trust, love, and fear God with one's whole heart, not to tempt God, etc.? Furthermore, what rules can be more just and holy than those which Moses ordains concerning the external worship of God, government, and love of one's neighbor?

Since there cannot be another word beyond the perfect teaching of the Law unless it were the Word of grace, it follows that this Prophet will not be a teacher of the Law but a minister of grace.

Lectures on Deuteronomy (1523–25)
LW 9, 176–77

You shall heed such a prophet.
Deuteronomy 18:15b

Thursday

Unless that new Prophet were to bring another word, Moses would not need to compare Him to himself when he says: "The Lord will raise Him up, like me." All the other prophets who taught Moses were not like Moses or similar to Moses but inferior to Moses, teaching what Moses had commanded. Therefore in all of them the people did not hear anyone else but Moses himself and his words. For Moses speaks in them; they are his mouth to the people. This Prophet, however, Moses dare not subordinate to himself and put his words into His mouth. He places Him above all prophets who taught on the basis of Moses. Unless He were greater than Moses, Moses would not yield obedience and authority to Him. Moreover, unless He taught greater things, He could not be greater.

Here we have those two ministries of the Word which are necessary for the salvation of the human race: the ministry of the Law and the ministry of the Gospel. The ministry of Moses is temporary, finally to be ended by the coming of the ministry of Christ, as he says here, "Heed Him." But the ministry of Christ will be ended by nothing else, since it brings eternal righteousness and "puts an end to sin," as it is said in Dan. 9:24.

The sin and wrath which Moses arouses through his ministry, that Prophet cancels through righteousness and grace by His ministry. This Prophet, therefore, demands nothing; but He grants what Moses demands.

Lectures on Deuteronomy (1523–25)
LW 9, 177–78

Friday

Moses was one hundred twenty years old when he died; his sight was unimpaired and his vigor had not abated.
Deuteronomy 34:7

The endurance of sight and strength in Moses signifies, according to the allegorical meaning, that the power of the Law does not grow less through length of days or magnitude of deeds; but it always oppresses and rouses guilty consciences until it dies, that is, until it is done away with through Christ and the new ministry of grace is established.

Finally, Moses is praised for his greatness (vv. 10ff.). After him no one equaled the great signs done in Egypt and in the desert through him. Especially did he stand out, however, because the Lord knew him face to face; that is, he lived and talked familiarly with God. But all his successors taught what Moses taught and were taught by him and from him, as the lesser ones. At the same time it remains true, as is said in chapter 18:18, that after Moses Another was to be raised up like Moses, namely, Christ. To Him the great Moses yielded, as to One far greater in worth and power, as we saw there. It also signifies this, that nothing greater can be taught and transmitted, so far as laws are concerned, than the Law of Moses. For all things reach their climax in him, except that the great Law was to give way to the even greater Gospel.

Lectures on Deuteronomy (1523–25)
LW 9, 310–11

SPRING

LAW AND GOSPEL

Oh, behold, my Lord Jesus Christ, my misery; needy and poor am I and yet so loathe to accept your remedy that I do not sigh for the riches of your grace. Set aflame in me, O Lord, the desire for your grace and faith in your promise that I may not offend you, my most gracious God, by my perverse unbelief and satiety. Amen.

What Luther Says, 3:1103, #3522

Law and Gospel

Monday

The law indeed was given through Moses; grace and truth came through Jesus Christ.
John 1:17

It is proper that the Law and God's Commandments provide me with the correct directives for life; they supply me with abundant information about righteousness and eternal life. The Law is a sermon which points me to life, and it is essential to remember this instruction. But it must be borne in mind that the Law does not *give* me life. It resembles a hand which directs me to the right road. The hand gives me the proper direction, but it will not conduct my steps along the way.

Thus the Law serves to indicate the will of God, and it leads us to a realization that we cannot keep it. It also acquaints us with human nature, with its capabilities, and with its limitations. The Law was given to us for the revelation of sin; but it does not have the power to save us from sin and rid us of it. It holds a mirror before us; we peer into it and perceive that we are devoid of righteousness and life. And this image impels us to cry: "Oh, come, Lord Jesus Christ, help us and give us grace to enable us to fulfill the Law's demands!"

Sermons on the Gospel of St. John (1537–40)
LW 22, 143–44

Tuesday

But now we are discharged from the law,
dead to that which held us captive, so that
we are slaves not under the old written
code but in the new life of the Spirit.
Romans 7:6

But how are we "discharged from the Law"? Doubtless because through faith in Christ we satisfy the demands of the Law and through grace are freed and voluntarily perform the works of the Law. But those who do not have this faith are active in works unwillingly and almost in fear or in a desire for their own convenience. Therefore love is necessary, which seeks the things of God, love which is given to them who ask in faith and in the name of Jesus.

Even though we sin often and are not perfectly voluntary, yet we have made a beginning and are progressing, and we are righteous and free. But we must constantly beware that we not fall back under the Law. For who knows whether or not they are acting out of fear or a love for their own convenience even in a very subtle manner in their devotional life and their good works, looking for a rest and a reward rather than the will of God?

Therefore we must always remain in faith and pray for love.

Lectures on Romans (1515–16)
LW 25, 59–60

Law and Gospel

Wednesday

He said to them, "Go into all the world and proclaim the good news to the whole creation." Mark 16:15

Gospel" [*Euangelium*] is a Greek word and means in Greek a good message, good tidings, good news, a good report, which one sings and tells with gladness. For example, when David overcame the great Goliath, there came among the Jewish people the good report and encouraging news that their terrible enemy had been struck down and that they had been rescued and given joy and peace. They sang and danced and were glad for it (1 Sam. 18:6).

Thus this gospel of God or New Testament is a good story and report, sounded forth into all the world by the apostles, telling of a true David who strove with sin, death, and the devil, and overcame them, and thereby rescued all those who were captive in sin, afflicted with death, and overpowered by the devil. Without any merit of their own he made them righteous, gave them life, and saved them, so that they were given peace and brought back to God. For this they sing, and thank and praise God, and are glad forever, if only they believe firmly and remain steadfast in faith.

"Prefaces to the New Testament" (1522, revised 1546)
LW 35, 358

Thursday

He [Jesus] said to them, "Thus it is written, that the Messiah is to suffer and to rise from the dead on the third day, and that repentance and forgiveness of sins is to be proclaimed in his name to all nations, beginning from Jerusalem."
Luke 24:46-47

The gospel, then, is nothing but the preaching about Christ, Son of God and of David, true God and true human, who by his death and resurrection has overcome for us the sin, death, and hell of all who believe in him.

See to it, therefore, that you do not make a Moses out of Christ, or a book of laws and doctrines out of the gospel. For the gospel does not expressly demand works of our own by which we become righteous and are saved; indeed it condemns such works. Rather the gospel demands faith in Christ: that he has overcome for us sin, death and hell, and thus gives us righteousness, life, and salvation not through our works, but through his own works, death, and suffering, in order that we may avail ourselves of his death and victory as though we had done it ourselves.

"Prefaces to the New Testament" (1522, revised 1546)
LW 35, 360

Law and Gospel

Friday

On the last day of the festival, the great day, while Jesus was standing there, he cried out, "Let anyone who is thirsty come to me."   John 7:37

This is the thirst which is not appeased until Christ appears and says: "If you would like to be content and enjoy peace of mind and a good conscience, I advise you to come to Me. Give up Moses and your works. Learn the difference between Me and Moses. Your thirst you got from Moses. His role and his office were to frighten you and to make you thirsty. But now come to Me, believe in Me, hear My doctrine. I am a different type of Preacher; I will give you drink and refresh you."

A person who masters the art of exact distinction between the Law and the Gospel should be called a real theologian. These two must be kept apart. The function of the Law is to frighten people and drive them to despair until they realize their inability to meet the demands of the Law or to obtain grace.

But Christ says: "Accept this from Me. You lack piety, but I have kept the Law for you. Your sins are forgiven." Both the Law and the Gospel must be taught and considered. It is a mistake to confine yourself to one of the two. The Law serves no other purpose than to create a thirst and to frighten the heart. The Gospel alone satisfies the thirst, makes us cheerful, and revives and consoles the conscience. Lest the teaching of the Gospel create lazy, gluttonous Christians who think they need not perform good works, the Law tells the old Adam: "Refrain from sin! Be pious! Desist from this, and do that!" Then, when the conscience becomes depressed and realizes that the Law is not a mere cipher, one becomes frightened. And then one must give ear to the voice of the Gospel. When you have sinned, hearken to the Teacher, Christ, who says: "Come to Me! I will not let you die of thirst but will give you drink."

Sermons on the Gospel of St. John (1530–32)
LW 23, 271–72

CHRIST'S PASSION

Almighty Father, eternal God, who did allow your Son to suffer the agony of the cross so that you might drive from us the enemy's power: Grant that we may so observe his passion and give thanks for it that we may thereby obtain forgiveness of sin and redemption from death eternal. Through the same your Son Jesus Christ our Lord. Amen.

LW 53, 133

Christ's Passion

Monday

Then Pilate took Jesus and had him flogged.... Then [Pilate] handed him over to them to be crucified.   John 19:1, 16

Dear friends, you know that it is customary in this season to preach on the Passion, so I have no doubt that you have heard many times what kind of passion and suffering it was. You have also heard why it was that God the Father ordained it, namely, that through it he wanted to help, not the person of Christ, for Christ had no need at all for this suffering. But we and the whole human race needed this suffering. Thus it was a gift which was given and presented to us out of pure grace and mercy.

"Sermon on Cross and Suffering, Preached at Coburg" (1530)
LW 51, 197–98

A great number of people followed him,   # Tuesday
and among them were women who were
beating their breasts and wailing for him.
But Jesus turned to them and said,
"Daughters of Jerusalem, do not weep for
me, but weep for yourselves and for your
children."   Luke 23:27-28

Some people meditate on Christ's passion by venting their anger on the Jews. This singing and ranting about wretched Judas satisfies them for they are in the habit of complaining about other people, of condemning and reproaching their adversaries. That might well be a meditation on the wickedness of Judas but not on the sufferings of Christ.

Some feel pity for Christ, lamenting and bewailing his innocence. They are like the women who followed Christ from Jerusalem and were chided and told by Christ that it would be better to weep for themselves and their children.

But they who contemplate Christ's passion aright view it with a terror-stricken heart and a despairing conscience. This terror must be felt as you witness the stern wrath and the unchanging earnestness with which God looks upon sin and sinners, so much so that he was unwilling to release sinners even for his only and dearest Son without his payment of the severest penalty for them.

"A Meditation on Christ's Passion" (1519)
LW 42, 7–9

Wednesday

For he was ... stricken for the transgression of my people.   Isaiah 53:8

If the dearest child is punished thus, what will be the fate of sinners? And if you seriously consider that it is God's very own Son, the eternal wisdom of the Father, who suffers, you will be terrified indeed. The more you think about it, the more intensely will you be frightened.

We must give ourselves wholly to this matter, for the main benefit of Christ's passion is that people see into their own true self and that they be terrified and crushed by this. Unless we seek that knowledge, we do not derive much benefit from Christ's passion. The real and true work of Christ's passion is to make us conformable to Christ, so that our conscience is tormented by our sins in the like measure as Christ was pitiably tormented in body and soul by our sins. This does not call for many words but for profound reflection and a great awe of sins.

"A Meditation on Christ's Passion" (1519)
LW 42, 9–10

Thursday

*But he was wounded for our transgres-
sions, crushed for our iniquities; upon him
was the punishment that made us whole,
and by his bruises we are healed.*
Isaiah 53:5

One who is so hardhearted and callous as not to be terrified by Christ's passion and led to a knowledge of self, has reason to fear. For it is inevitable, whether in this life or in hell, that you will have to become conformable to Christ's image and suffering. You should pray God to soften your heart and let you now ponder Christ's passion with profit to you. Unless God inspires our heart, it is impossible for us of ourselves to meditate thoroughly on Christ's passion. You must first seek God's grace and ask that it be accomplished by his grace and not by your own power.

We say without hesitation that one who contemplates God's sufferings for a day, an hour, yes, only a quarter of an hour, does better than to fast a whole year, pray a psalm daily, yes better than to hear a hundred masses. This meditation changes one's being and, almost like baptism, gives one a new birth. Here the passion of Christ performs its natural and noble work, strangling the old Adam and banishing all joy, delight, and confidence which one could derive from other creatures, even as Christ was forsaken by all, even by God.

After people have thus become aware of their sin and are terrified in their hearts, they must watch that sin does not remain in their consciences, for this would lead to sheer despair. Just as our knowledge of sin flowed from Christ and was acknowledged by us, so we must pour this sin back on him and free our conscience of it. Sin cannot remain on Christ, since it is swallowed up by his resurrection.

"A Meditation on Christ's Passion" (1519)
LW 42, 10–12

Friday

Since therefore Christ suffered in the flesh, arm yourselves also with the same intention (for whoever has suffered in the flesh has finished with sin).   1 Peter 4:1

First of all, you must no longer contemplate the suffering of Christ (for this has already done its work and terrified you), but pass beyond that and see his friendly heart and how this heart beats with such love for you that it impels him to bear with pain your conscience and your sin. Then your heart will be filled with love for him, and the confidence of your faith will be strengthened.

After your heart has thus become firm in Christ, and love, not fear of pain, has made you a foe of sin, then Christ's passion must from that day on become a pattern for your entire life. If pain or sickness afflicts you, consider how paltry this is in comparison with the thorny crown and nails of Christ. If you are obliged to do or to refrain from doing things against your wishes, ponder how Christ was bound and captured and led hither and yon. If you are beset by pride, see how your Lord was mocked and ridiculed along with criminals. If unchastity and lust assail you, remember how ruthlessly Christ's tender flesh was scourged, pierced, and beaten. If hatred, envy, and vindictiveness beset you, recall that Christ, who indeed had more reason to avenge himself, interceded with tears and cries for you and for all his enemies.

So then, this is how we can draw strength and encouragement from Christ against every vice and failing. That is a proper contemplation of Christ's passion, and such are its fruits.

"A Meditation on Christ's Passion" (1519)
LW 42, 13–14

THE CROSS

May our dear Lord Jesus Christ show you his hands and his side and gladden your heart with his love, and may you behold and hear only him until you find your joy in him. Amen.

Letters, 117

The Cross

Monday

"Whoever does not take up the cross and follow me is not worthy of me."
Matthew 10:38

We must note in the first place that Christ by his suffering not only saved us from the devil, death, and sin, but also that his suffering is an example, which we are to follow in our suffering. Though our suffering and cross should never be so exalted that we think we can be saved by it or earn the least merit through it, nevertheless we should suffer after Christ, that we may be conformed to him. For God has appointed that we should not only believe in the crucified Christ, but also be crucified with him, as He clearly shows in the above Scripture and in many places in the Gospels: "If they have called the master of the house Beelzebul, how much more will they malign those of his household" (Matt. 10:25). Therefore every Christian must be aware that suffering will not fail to come.

Beyond this, it should be the kind of suffering which we have not chosen ourselves, as the fanatics choose their own suffering. It should be the kind of suffering which, if it were possible, we would gladly be rid of, suffering visited upon us by the devil or the world. Then what is needed is to hold fast and submit oneself to it, as I have said, namely, that one know that we must suffer, in order that we may thus be conformed to Christ, and that it cannot be otherwise, that everyone must have his cross and suffering.

"Sermon on Cross and Suffering, Preached at Coburg" (1530)
LW 51, 198–99

Tuesday

By his great mercy he has given us a new birth into a living hope through the resurrection of Jesus Christ from the dead, and into an inheritance that is imperishable, undefiled, and unfading. . . . In this you rejoice, even if now for a little while you have had to suffer various trials.
1 Peter 1:3b-4a, 6

The cause of our suffering is the same as that for which all the saints have suffered from the beginning. Of course the whole world must bear witness that we are not suffering because of public scandal or vice, such as adultery, fornication, murder, and the like. Rather we suffer because we hold to the Word of God, preach it, hear it, learn it, and practice it. And since this is the cause of our suffering, so let it always be; we have the same promise and the same cause for suffering which all the saints have always had. We too can comfort ourselves with the same promise and cling to it in our suffering and tribulation, as is highly necessary.

So in our suffering we should so act that we give our greatest attention to the promise, in order that our cross and affliction may be turned to good, to something which we could never have asked or thought. And this is precisely the thing which makes a difference between the Christian's suffering and afflictions and those of all other people. For they also have their afflictions, cross, and misfortune, just as they also have their times when they can sit in the rose garden and employ their good fortune and their goods as they please. But when they run into affliction and suffering, they have nothing to comfort them, for they do not have the mighty promises and confidence in God which Christians have. Therefore they cannot comfort themselves with the assurance that God will help them to bear the affliction, much less can they count on it that he will turn their affliction and suffering to good.

"Sermon on Cross and Suffering, Preached at Coburg" (1530)
LW 51, 200–1

Wednesday

For many live as enemies of the cross of Christ; I have often told you of them, and now I tell you even with tears.
Philippians 3:18

This is clear: Those who do not know Christ do not know God hidden in suffering. Therefore they prefer works to suffering, glory to the cross, strength to weakness, wisdom to folly, and in general, good to evil. These are the people whom the apostle calls "enemies of the cross of Christ" for they hate the cross and suffering and love works and the glory of works. Thus they call the good of the cross evil and the evil of a deed good. God can be found only in suffering and the cross, as has already been said. Therefore the friends of the cross say that the cross is good and works are evil, for through the cross works are dethroned and the old Adam, who is especially edified by works, is crucified. It is impossible for believers not to be puffed up by their good works unless they have first been deflated and destroyed by suffering and evil until they know that they are worthless and that their works are not theirs but God's.

"Heidelberg Disputation" (1518)
LW 31, 53

"My God, my God, why have you forsaken me?"   Matthew 27:46b

Thursday

You must look at sin only within the picture of grace. The picture of grace is nothing else but that of Christ on the cross and of all his dear saints.

How is that to be understood? Grace and mercy are there where Christ on the cross takes your sin from you, bears it for you, and destroys it. To believe this firmly, to keep it before your eyes and not to doubt it, means to view the picture of Christ and to engrave it in yourself. Here sins are never sins, for here they are overcome and swallowed up in Christ. He takes your death upon himself and strangles it so that it may not harm you, if you believe that he does it for you and see your death in him and not in yourself. Likewise, he also takes your sins upon himself and overcomes them with his righteousness out of sheer mercy, and if you believe that, your sins will never work you harm.

So then, gaze at the heavenly picture of Christ, who descended into hell (1 Pet. 3:19) for your sake and was forsaken by God as one eternally damned when he spoke the words on the cross, "Eli, Eli, lama sabachthani!"—"My God, my God, why hast thou forsaken me?" (Matt. 27:46). In that picture your hell is defeated and your uncertain election is made sure. If you concern yourself solely with that and believe that it was done for you, you will surely be preserved in this same faith. Never, therefore, let this be erased from your vision. Seek yourself only in Christ and not in yourself and you will find yourself in him eternally.

"A Sermon on Preparing to Die" (1519)
LW 42, 104–6

The Cross

Friday

He will drink from the stream by the path.
Psalm 110:7a

In this life, the prophet says, He will "drink from the brook [stream]";
that is He will suffer and die. By "drink" or "cup" Scripture means
any sort of torture, misery, and suffering just as Christ prayed in the
garden, where He sweat blood (Luke 22:44) and said (Matt. 26:39):
"Dear Father, if it is possible, remove this cup from Me. But if it
cannot be otherwise but that I drink it, Thy will be done."

But here we do not have the simple expression "drink of the
cup," as in other places. "He will drink from the brook" is intended
to show that He will not feel ordinary or small pains and misery; but
He will bear or endure the greatest, the most bitter and cruel pain
and torture, and will die a most contemptible death. For the word
"torrent" refers to a strong and fast-flowing stream or brook, which,
when it is swollen from heavy rains, tears irresistibly onward in full
flood. So the suffering of Christ is not called a mere drink or cupful
but means drinking up an entire stream or brook, as Psalm 42:7 also
says of such suffering: "All Thy waves and all Thy billows have gone
over me." This stream, then, is the whole world with its power. Lastly,
we should mention the devil and all his hell, sin, the terror and fear
of death, and whatever other miseries exist. All this came upon Him;
He had to drink it up and conquer.

Commentary on "Psalm 110" (1535)
LW 13, 345–46

RESURRECTION

Grant, dear Lord God, that the blessed Day of your holy advent may come soon, so that we may be redeemed from this bad, wicked world, the devil's dominion, and be freed from the terrible plague which we must suffer from without and within, from wicked people and our own conscience. Do dispatch this old maggot sack that we may finally get a different body, which is not full of sin, inclined to unchasteness and to everything evil, as the present one is, but one that is redeemed from all bodily and spiritual misery and made like unto your glorious body, dear Lord Jesus Christ, that we may at last come to our glorious redemption. Amen.

What Luther Says, 3:1108–9, #3542

Resurrection

Monday

[Jesus our Lord] was handed over to death for our trespasses and was raised for our justification.   Romans 4:25

Now we come to the resurrection of Christ, to the day of Easter. After a person has contemplated the passion and cross of Christ and has thus become aware of his sin and is terrified in his heart, he must watch that sin does not remain in his conscience, for this would lead to sheer despair.

You cast your sins from yourself and onto Christ when you firmly believe that his wounds and sufferings are your sins, to be borne and paid for by him, as we read in Isaiah 53:6, "The Lord has laid on him the iniquity of us all." St. Peter says, "in his body has he borne our sins on the wood of the cross" (1 Pet. 2:24). You must stake everything on these and similar verses. But if you behold your sin resting on Christ and see it overcome by his resurrection, and then boldly believe this, even it is dead and nullified. Sin cannot remain on Christ, since it is swallowed up in his resurrection. Now you see no wounds, no pain in him, and no sign of sin. Thus St. Paul declares that "Christ died for our sin and rose for our justification." That is to say, in his suffering Christ makes our sin known and thus destroys it, but through his resurrection he justifies us and delivers us from all sin, if we believe this.

"A Meditation on Christ's Passion" (1519)
LW 42, 12

We know that Christ, being raised from the dead, will never die again; death no longer has dominion over him.
Romans 6:9

Behold Jesus Christ, the King of glory, rising from the dead. Here the heart can find its supreme joy and lasting possessions. Here there is not the slightest trace of evil, for "Christ being risen from the dead, will not die again. Death no longer has dominion over him." Here is that furnace of love and the fire of God in Zion, as Isaiah says, for Christ is not only born to us, but also given to us [Isa. 9:6]. Therefore, his resurrection and everything that he accomplished through it are mine. In Romans 8:32 the Apostle exults in exuberant joy, "Has he not also given me all things with him?"

What is it that he has wrought by his resurrection? He has destroyed sin and raised up righteousness, abolished death and restored life, conquered hell and bestowed everlasting glory on us. These blessings are so incalculable that the human mind hardly dares believe that they have been granted to us. I am a sinner, but I am borne by his righteousness which is given to me. I am unclean, but his holiness is my sanctification, in which I ride gently. I am an ignorant fool, but his wisdom carries me forward. I deserve condemnation, but I am set free by his redemption.

"Fourteen Consolations" (1520)
LW 42, 163–64

Wednesday

Then the LORD replied to [Moses], ". . . I will raise up from them a prophet like you from among their own people; I will put my words in the mouth of the prophet, who shall speak to them everything I command." Deuteronomy 18:17-18

This statement and others like it perpetuated the confident faith in the coming of Christ the Messiah among the Jewish people. They waited for the One who, as Moses had said in this passage, would teach them everything. In this faith they died. They were saved as well as we are, who now believe that Christ ascended to heaven and sits at the right hand of His Father, that He will raise us from the dead on the Last Day and make us more radiant and resplendent than the sun, that He will judge the quick and the dead, that He will save all believers, and that He will also raise the body from the grave. Although we must all die before we experience this, we are firmly persuaded and believe that it will come to pass. In this confidence we die; and by this faith we are saved, although we do not yet understand just how it will happen. But even though we do not see this, grasp it, or understand it, nonetheless we know that whoever believes will be saved.

Similarly, we take hold of eternal life by faith today, although we do not really understand what it is. We believe that one day we shall partake of it.

Sermons on the Gospel of St. John (1537–40)
LW 22, 285

I will raise them up on the last day.
John 6:54b

Thursday

You must not judge by external appearances. You must be guided by the Word which promises and gives you everlasting life. Then you truly have eternal life.

Even though your senses tell you otherwise, this does not matter. This does not mean that you have forfeited life, for sickness, death, perils, and sin which assail you will not devour or finish you. They will have to leave you in peace. They do not weaken or kill Christ. When these all have passed and have left you constant in your faith, then you will see what you have believed.

But you retort: "The fact remains that I must die."

This makes no difference! Go ahead and die in God's name. You are still assured of eternal life; it will surely be yours. To die, to be buried, to have people tread on your grave, to be consumed by worms—all this will not matter to you. It is certain that Christ will raise you up again. For here you have His promise: "I will raise you up."

Therefore your eyes will behold what your faith so confidently relied on.

Sermons on the Gospel of St. John (1530–32)
LW 23, 131

Resurrection

Friday

... the hope of eternal life that God, who never lies, promised before the ages began.
Titus 1:2

This is also a word of confidence, because he is speaking against those who are timid and weak in faith when he says "who does not lie." For to believe that in hope one has a life that is eternal, this passes all understanding (Phil. 4:7), even that of the godly. The ungodly ridicule this proclamation when they hear it. But the godly strive to believe this, because it is the greatest of doctrines to believe in eternal life.

Thus the weak should be buoyed up with these words: "Do you not think that He will live up to what He has said?" Thus Christ gives the consolation in Luke 12:32: "Fear not, O little flock." This consolation has always been necessary for all believers; for if people look about them, they stumble at the idea of eternal life. Our primary impression is that we are sinners, but it is a sublime thing to believe that God has prepared eternal life. He raises the poor up from the dirt and leads them from sin and death; He crowns the unworthy. Thus He says in John 14:1-2: "Let not your heart be troubled. In My Father's house, do not doubt. Eternal life is promised to you. It is a grand thing, but do not fear. You are a little flock, but you should have the courage to believe; for it has pleased the Father. Besides, if dwelling places were not prepared, I would prepare them for you now."

"Lectures on Titus" (1527)
LW 29, 11–12

JOY

Grant that anger or other bitterness does not reign over us, but that by your grace, genuine kindness, loyalty, and every kind of friendliness, generosity, and gentleness may reign in us. Grant that inordinate sadness and depression may not prevail in us, but let joy and delight in your grace and mercy come over us. Amen.

LW 43, 32

Monday

Thus he has given us, through these things, his precious and very great promises, so that through them you may escape from the corruption that is in the world because of lust, and may become participants of the divine nature.   2 Peter 1:4

Through the power of faith, he says, we partake of and have association or communion with the divine nature. This is a verse without a parallel in the New and the Old Testament, even though unbelievers regard it as a trivial matter that we partake of the divine nature itself. But what is the divine nature? It is eternal truth, righteousness, wisdom, everlasting life, peace, joy, happiness, and whatever can be called good. Now those who become partakers of the divine nature receive all this, so that they live eternally and have everlasting peace, joy, and happiness, and are pure, clean, righteous, and almighty against the devil, sin, and death.

Therefore this is what Peter wants to say: Just as God cannot be deprived of being eternal life and eternal truth, so you cannot be deprived of this. If anything is done to you, it must be done to God; for the person who wants to oppress a Christian must oppress God.

"Sermons on the Second Epistle of St. Peter" (ca. 1523)
LW 30, 155

Serve the Lord with fear, and rejoice with **Tuesday**
trembling.
Psalm 2:11 (Luther's translation)

The true fear of God is a filial fear, that is, a fear mixed with joy or hope. But if you follow your feeling, you will perceive that joy is all but overwhelmed and extinguished by fear. But you must not on that account let your heart sink or despair, but trust in the Lord and lay hold on his Word, which declares that God's anger is but for a moment (Ps. 30:5) and His favor is for a lifetime. That is, God wants us to live. He does not want us to perish. And for this very reason He sends us blows. And so it happens that you feel at least some small drop of joy. It will grow little by little until it finally overcomes fear. The practice is difficult, but is nevertheless of the kind which the saints of God learned to do, as their examples show. Moreover, the Holy Spirit will come to our aid, especially when we pray.

There is an important reason why He unites joy with trembling. If one feels pure joy, smugness follows; presumption follows smugness, and damnation follows presumption. For God cannot tolerate presumption. We shall, however, mix these in such a way if we rejoice in God but are disturbed within ourselves. For we are not only foolish but also miserable sinners. There is cause enough, then for us to tremble and fear.

But we should fear in such a way that joy is not entirely excluded. It must, moreover, be true joy. For it will not be so shut up within the heart that no signs of it will appear outside. A quiet heart and one which truly believes that God has been reconciled to us on account of Christ will produce a cheerful countenance and happy eyes; it will loosen the tongue for the praises to God.

Commentary on "Psalm 2" (1532)
LW 12, 78–79, 81

Wednesday

*Restore to me the joy of your salvation,
and sustain in me a willing spirit.
Psalm 51:12*

This is now the third gift of the Holy Spirit that he asks to be conferred upon him. It is surely a fine sequence that the prophet follows; as though he were to say, "I am already righteous by the grace of God, because I am sure of the forgiveness of sins. Then I am also sanctified. Now a third still remains, that there come a courageous and strong mind which will confess this justifier and sanctifier before the world and will not let itself be driven away from confession by any dangers."

For this reason we have rendered this verse in German in such a way that he appears to ask for a mind that is "happy" and despises all dangers. "Happiness" here properly means constancy or a fearless mind that is not afraid of the world or Satan or even death. Such a mind we see in Paul, when he says with a happy, exulting, and full spirit (Rom. 8:35): "Who shall separate us from the love of God?" It seems to me that in this passage David is asking for the same thing, that he might be able to confess his God freely, despising all the dangers of the world.

When he says, "Restore to me the joy," he means that he had almost been broken by these dangers. For this reason he prays that this joy might be restored, the joy of God's salvation. That is, he wants his mind to be confirmed in such a way that he will not doubt the presence of God and His will to save in the dangers which confession brings with it.

Commentary on "Psalm 51" (1532)
LW 12, 382–83

May the God of hope fill you with all joy and peace in believing, so that you may abound in hope by the power of the Holy Spirit.   Romans 15:13

Thursday

Joy is a trusting conscience and peace, mutual concord. The apostle puts joy first and then peace, because joy makes believers peaceful and composed in themselves. When they have become composed, it is easy for them to make peace with others. But those who are sad and disturbed are easily upset at others and of a stormy mind.

All these things take place "in believing," because our joy and peace do not consist in something material, but are beyond material things, in hope. Otherwise the God of hope would not give them, for He gives good things which are hidden, joy in sadness and personal affliction, peace in the midst of tumult and outward persecution. Where faith is lacking, a person falls in sadness and persecution, because material things, in which he had placed his trust while they were available, fail him. But persecution causes hope to abound, as he said in chapter 5:4: "Trial produces hope."

And this is "by the power of the Holy Spirit." It is not because we trust in our own abilities that "trial produces hope." Then we would still be weak and powerless under persecutions. But "the Spirit helps us in our weakness," so that we cannot only hold out but be made perfect and triumphant.

Lectures on Romans (1515–16)
LW 25, 518

Friday

Sing to God, play psalters to His name. Pave the way for Him who rides in Araboth. His name is the LORD, be of good cheer before his face.
Psalm 68:4 (Luther's translation)

To pave the way" is to improve a bad, swampy, and bottomless road that is full of debris, fagots, and stones—to make a previously impassable road fit for travel. This refers to human hearts. The evil, foul, and bottomless quagmires of their various evil tendencies once made them entirely unfit for the paths of God.

But the Gospel and the proclamation of God's name in Christ do construct a solid highway, for faith furnishes a good foundation and dries out every foul marsh of the wicked flesh. And now Christ rides on them; that is, He performs in them His works, which are love, joy, peace, kindness, meekness, chastity (Gal. 5:22). Let us note the word "ride." He does not stand still; for the life in faith implies progress, a walk or journey toward heaven into another life. Thus the believer possesses peace and joy before God and is of good cheer.

Commentary on "Psalm 68" (1521)
LW 13, 4–6

PEACE

*Lord God, heavenly Father, who creates holy desire, good
counsel, and right works: Give to your servants peace which the
world cannot give so that our hearts may cling to your
commandments, and that by your protection we may live our
days quietly and secure from our enemies; through Jesus Christ
your Son our Lord. Amen.*

LW 53, 138

Monday

Therefore, since we are justified by faith, we have peace with God through our Lord Jesus Christ.   Romans 5:1

In this letter the apostle speaks as one who is extremely happy and full of joy. In the entire Scripture there is scarcely another text like this chapter, scarcely one so expressive. For he describes the grace and mercy of God in the clearest possible manner, telling us what it is like and how great it is for us.

Note how he begins, placing this spiritual peace with God only after righteousness has preceded it. For first he says, "since we have been justified through faith," and then, "we have peace." But the perversity of men seeks peace before righteousness, and for this reason they do not find peace. Thus the apostle creates a very fine antithesis in these words, namely,

The righteous man has peace with God but affliction in the world, because he lives in the Spirit.

The unrighteous man has peace with the world but affliction and tribulation with God, because he lives in the flesh.

But as the Spirit is eternal, so also will be the peace of the righteous man and the tribulation of the unrighteous.

And as the flesh is temporal, so will be the tribulation of the righteous and the peace of the unrighteous.

Lectures on Romans (1515–16)
LW 25, 43, 285–86

He grants peace within your borders; he fills you with the finest of wheat.
Psalm 147:14

Tuesday

The third blessing named in this psalm is peace, that there is not only protection and prosperity in the city, but peace and good times in the countryside round about. There people are able to live in safety, plow, plant, raise cattle, or carry on other activities. And this peace includes loyal neighbors and an obedient nobility.

Of course, it is true, as I said before, that we should do our utmost to make peace prevail in our country, just as we should plow and sow to raise grain. To keep the peace, we should also be patient and friendly toward our neighbors. And our rulers should establish borders, build roads, and arm themselves against enemies and evil neighbors. But when all this has been done, one should say: "Well, I have done everything necessary to keep the peace, and all that is required for defense. But all this is nothing. Lord God, give Thou Thy blessing to this work, and establish peace within our borders."

But where are those who give thanks to God for this gift of peace? Yes, where are those who even recognize it as a God-given gift or do not, on top of everything else, show contempt for God? We exploit Him for our own pleasure and liking, and act as though such a peace were our birthright in which to live and act as we choose, against both God and humanity.

Commentary on "Psalm 147" (1531)
LW 14, 117–20

Wednesday

The one who thus serves Christ is acceptable to God and has human approval.
Romans 14:18

First one ought to be acceptable to God because of one's righteousness which is by faith. Then one ought to be approved by other people because of one's peacefulness. For one ought to seek not one's own things but the neighbor's good.

Hence it is common to say of those who are restless and who disturb others that they do not have peace, because they will not allow others to live their lives in peace, but they disturb them. These people the apostle calls restless, 1 Thess. 5:12-14: "Be at peace with those who are over you, rebuke the restless, encourage the fainthearted, help the weak, be patient with them all." Those who are restless and disturb the peace are not "approved by others," but are displeasing to them.

Thus the apostle would have us not only be at peace but also bring peace, be quiet and modest toward one another. For he then says: "Let us then pursue what makes for peace" (v. 19), that is, those things which do not disturb others but which edify and calm them. And what are these things? The answer is: Love teaches us what they are as the time and the place require. For they cannot be given to us in the particular.

Lectures on Romans (1515–16)
LW 25, 505

Blessed are the dead who from now on die
in the Lord.   Revelation 14:13b

Thursday

You must not view or ponder death as such, not in yourself or in your nature. If you do that you will be lost and defeated. But you must resolutely turn your gaze, the thoughts of your heart, and all your senses away from this picture and look at death closely and untiringly only as seen in those who died in God's grace and who have overcome death, particularly in Christ and then also in all his saints.

In such pictures death will not appear terrible and gruesome. No, it will seem contemptible and dead, slain and overcome in life. For Christ is nothing other than sheer life, as his saints are likewise. The more profoundly you impress that image upon your heart and gaze upon it, the more the image of death will pale and vanish of itself without struggle or battle. Thus your heart will be at peace and you will be able to die calmly in Christ and with Christ, as we read in Revelation, "Blessed are they who die in the Lord Christ." This was foreshown in the Old Testament where we hear that when the children of Israel were bitten by fiery serpents they did not struggle with these serpents, but merely had to raise their eyes to the dead bronze serpent and the living ones dropped from them by themselves and perished. Thus you must concern yourself solely with the death of Christ and then you will find life. But if you look at death in any other way, it will kill you with great anxiety and anguish. This is why Christ says, "In the world—that is, in yourselves—you have unrest, but in me you will find peace" (John 16:33).

"A Sermon on Preparing to Die" (1519)
LW 42, 104

Friday

Peace I leave with you; my peace I give to you. I do not give to you as the world gives. Do not let your hearts be troubled, and do not let them be afraid.
John 14:27

It is a very comforting and pleasing bequest that He leaves them. It does not consist of cities and castles or of silver and gold. It is peace, the greatest treasure in heaven and on earth. He does not want His disciples to be fearful and mournful. He wants them to have true, beautiful, and longed-for peace of heart.

"For so far as I am concerned," Christ says, "you shall have nothing but sheer peace and joy. All My sermons to you and all My associations with you have let you see and realize that I love you with all My heart and do for you everything that is good, and that My Father is most graciously disposed toward you. That is the best I can leave to you and give you, for peace of heart is the greatest peace. Hence the expression, 'Joy of heart exceeds all other joy, sadness of heart surpasses all other woe.' I am leaving you this precious and great treasure: a good, fine, and peaceful heart toward God and Me. For I am leaving you the Father's and My love and friendship. You have seen and heard nothing but kind and friendly words and works from Me. And these are not Mine; they are the Father's. Thus you possess everything you could desire from Me, even though I am leaving you and you see Me no more."

Sermons on the Gospel of St. John (1537)
LW 24, 177–78

FAITH ALONE

The Father and God of all consolation grant you, through his holy Word and Spirit, a steadfast, joyful, and grateful faith blessedly to overcome this and all other trouble, and finally to taste and experience that what he himself says is true: "Be of good cheer; I have overcome the world." And with this I commend your body and soul to his mercy. Amen.

LW 50, 21

Faith Alone

Monday

Yet we know that a person is justified not by the works of the law but through faith in Jesus Christ. Galatians 2:16a

Christian faith is not an idle quality or an empty husk in the heart, which may exist in a state of mortal sin until love comes along to make it alive. But if it is true faith, it is a sure trust and firm acceptance in the heart. It takes hold of Christ in such a way that Christ is the object of faith, or rather not the object but, so to speak, the One who is present in the faith itself.

Thus faith is a sort of knowledge or darkness that nothing can see. Yet the Christ of whom faith takes hold is sitting in the darkness as God sat in the midst of darkness on Sinai and in the temple. Therefore our "formal righteousness" is not a love that informs faith; but it is faith itself, a cloud in our hearts, that is, trust in a thing we do not see, in Christ, who is present especially when He cannot be seen. Therefore faith justifies because it takes hold of and possesses this treasure, the present Christ.

Lectures on Galatians (1535)
LW 26, 129–30

So you are no longer a slave but a child, and if a child then also an heir, through God.   Galatians 4:7

Tuesday

It transcends all the capacity of the human mind when he says "heirs," not of some very wealthy and powerful king, but of Almighty God, the Creator of all. If someone could believe with a certain and constant faith, he could regard all the power and wealth of all the world as filth in comparison with his heavenly inheritance. For what is the whole world in comparison to heaven?

He would desire to depart and to be with Christ. Nothing more delightful could happen to him than a premature death, for he would know that it is the end of all his evils and that through it he comes into his inheritance. A person who believed this completely would not go on living very long. He would soon be consumed by his overwhelming joy.

But the law in our members at war with the law of our mind (Rom. 7:23) does not permit faith to be perfect. We need the aid and comfort of the Holy Spirit. Paul himself exclaims (Rom. 7:24): "Wretched man that I am! Who will deliver me from this body of death?" He did not always have pleasant and happy thoughts about his future inheritance in heaven. Over and over he experienced sadness of spirit and fear.

From this it is evident how difficult a thing faith is. For a perfect faith would soon bring a perfect contempt and scorn for this present life. We would not attach our hearts so firmly to physical things that their presence would give us confidence and their removal would produce dejection and even despair. But we would do everything with complete love, humility, and patience.

Lectures on Galatians (1535)
LW 26, 392–93

Faith Alone

Wednesday

For in Christ Jesus neither circumcision nor uncircumcision counts for anything; the only thing that counts is faith working through love.   Galatians 5:6

Here Paul presents the Christian life—faith that is neither imaginary nor hypocritical but true and living. It is a faith that arouses and motivates good works through love. He says: "It is true that faith alone justifies, without works. But I am speaking about genuine faith. After it has justified, it will not go to sleep but it is active through love."

Thus he describes the whole Christian life. Inwardly it is faith toward God, and outwardly it is love or works toward one's neighbor. In this way a person is a Christian in a total sense. Inwardly through faith in the sight of God, who does not need our works; outwardly in the sight of other people, who do not derive any benefit from our faith but do derive benefit from works or from our love.

Earlier Paul has discussed the internal nature of faith and has taught that it is righteousness or rather justification in the sight of God. Here he connects it with love and works; that is, he speaks of its external function. He says that it is the impulse and motivation of good works or of love toward one's neighbor. Thus it is true faith toward God, which loves and helps one's neighbor. This is the total life of Christians.

Lectures on Galatians (1535)
LW 27, 28, 30–31

Thursday

Therefore, since we are justified by faith, we have peace with God through our Lord Jesus Christ, through whom we have obtained access to this grace in which we stand; and we boast in our hope of sharing the glory of God.   Romans 5:1, 2

God in his grace has provided us with a Man in whom we may trust, rather than in our works. He wants us to rely on Christ so that we will not waver in ourselves nor be satisfied with the righteousness which has begun in us unless it cleaves to and flows from Christ's righteousness, and so that no fool, having once accepted the gift, will think himself already contented and secure. But he does not want us to halt in what has been received, but rather to draw near from day to day so that we may be fully transformed into Christ.

His righteousness is perpetual and sure; there is no change, there is there no lack, for he himself is the Lord of all. Therefore whenever Paul preached faith in Christ, he did so with the utmost care to proclaim that righteousness is not only through him or from him, but even that it is in him. He draws us into himself, and transforms us, and places us as if in hiding "until the wrath passes away" (Isa. 26:20). Observe, faith is not enough, but only the faith which hides under the wings of Christ and glories in His righteousness.

Paul teaches faith in such a way as to thrust it under the wings of Christ. Faith is precisely that which makes you a chick, and Christ a hen, so that you have hope under his wings. To have faith is to cleave to him, to presume on him, because he is holy and just for you.

"Against Latomus" (1521)
LW 32, 235–36

Faith Alone

Friday

The only thing that counts is faith working through love.   Galatians 5:6b

St. Paul does not speak here about what faith is or does by its own work (which he abundantly teaches earlier throughout the whole epistle), nor does he speak about what love is or does; rather, he briefly summarizes what an entire Christian life should be, namely, faith and love; faith in God, which apprehends Christ and receives forgiveness of sins apart from all works, and after that love toward the neighbor, which as the fruit of faith proves that faith is true and not lazy or false, but active and living. For that reason he does not say that love is active but, rather, that faith is active, that faith practices love and makes it active. St. Paul ascribes everything to faith which not only receives grace from God but also is active toward the neighbor and out of itself gives birth to and produces love or works.

Treatise on "The Private Mass and the Consecration of Priests" (1533)
LW 38, 184

LOVE

O sweetest Love, your grace on us bestow;
Set our hearts with sacred fire aglow,
That with hearts united we love each other,
Ev'ry stranger, sister, and brother.
        LBW #317 "To God the Holy Spirit Let Us Pray," v. 2

Love

Monday
"For I have come to call not the righteous but sinners."   Matthew 9:13b

God's love does not find, but creates, that which is pleasing to it. Human love comes into being through that which is pleasing to it. The second statement is clear and is accepted by all philosophers and theologians, for the object of love is its cause. For this reason human love avoids sinners and evil persons.

The first statement is clear because God's love which lives in man loves sinners, evil persons, fools, and weaklings in order to make them righteous, good, wise, and strong. Rather than seeking its own good, the love of God flows forth and bestows good. Therefore sinners are attractive because they are loved; they are not loved because they are attractive.

Thus Christ says: "For I came not to call the righteous, but sinners." This is the love of the cross, born of the cross, which turns in the direction where it does not find good which it may enjoy, but where it may confer good upon the bad and needy person.

"Heidelberg Disputation" (1518)
LW 31, 57

But when the goodness and loving kindness **Tuesday**
of God our Savior appeared, he saved us.
Titus 3:4, 5a

Here is a sweetness of life, not only goodness but also kindness. A man is kind or sweet when he is friendly and well-disposed, easily approachable, not harsh, but pleasant and joyful. He makes an effort to have people enjoy being about him. They are glad to hear him speak. He is companionable, affable, and easy for everyone to get along with. He is a brother to every man you can think of. This is a sweet manner. This text sets forth Christ as one who had the sweetness of golden virtue and of deity.

And goodness—that most gracious treatment of us and attitude toward us in Christ. Whoever was with Him preferred His company to that of the Pharisees. Paul is speaking about Christ's activity. He lived among us in the sweetest of ways, offended no one, and tolerated everyone. With this sweetness He did not serve Himself but sought to show love and the effects of love toward the blind by giving them sight. He was eager to serve people out of generosity and friendliness.

And now God is so disposed toward us in Christ. For it is Christ who treats us sweetly, who does everything to help us, who gives His gifts, who gives teachers to teach us and to help and strengthen us in bearing evils, who is present at death to receive our souls—in short, who wants to love people.

"Lectures on Titus" (1527)
LW 29, 78–79

Wednesday

*Now that you have purified your souls by
your obedience to the truth so that you
have genuine mutual love, love one
another deeply from the heart.*
1 Peter 1:22

The apostles Peter and Paul differentiate between brotherly love and love in general. Brotherhood means that Christians should all be like brothers and sisters and make no distinction among them; for since we all have one Christ in common, one Baptism, one faith, one treasure, I am no better than you are.

Thus in Baptism we Christians have all obtained one brotherhood. From this no saint has more than I and you. For I have been bought with just as high a price as he has been bought. God has spent just as much on me as He has spent on the greatest saint. We are brothers and sisters.

Love, however, is greater than brotherhood; for it extends also to enemies, and particularly to those who are not worthy of love. For just as faith is active where it sees nothing, so love should also not see anything and do its work chiefly where nothing lovable but only aversion and hostility is seen.

"Sermons on the First Epistle of St. Peter" (ca. 1523)
LW 30, 42–43

"This is my commandment, that you love one another as I have loved you."
John 15:12

Thursday

We shall now speak of the fruit of this sacrament of Holy Communion, which is love; that is, that we should treat our neighbor as God has treated us. Now we have received from God nothing but love and favor, for Christ has pledged and given us his righteousness and everything he has. He has poured out upon us all his treasures, which no mortal can measure and no angel can understand or fathom, for God is a glowing furnace of love, reaching even from the earth to the heavens.

Love, I say, is a fruit of this sacrament. But this I do not yet perceive among you here in Wittenberg, even though you have had much preaching and, after all, you ought to have carried this out in practice. This is the chief thing, which is the only business of a Christian. But nobody wants to be in this, though you want to practice all sorts of unnecessary things, which are of no account. If you do not want to show yourselves Christians by your love, then leave the other things undone, too, for St. Paul says in (1 Cor. 13:1), "If I speak in the tongues of mortals and of angels, but have not love, I am a noisy gong or a clanging cymbal."

You are willing to take all of God's goods in the sacrament, but you are not willing to pour them out again in love. Nobody extends a helping hand to another, nobody seriously considers the other person, but everyone looks out for himself and his own gain, insists on his own way, and lets everything else go hang.

"Eight Sermons at Wittenberg" (7th Sermon) (1522)
LW 51, 95–96

Friday

"Those who love me will be loved by my Father, and I will love them and reveal myself to them." John 14:21b

But what will those who have such love for Christ get in return? Where is the profit in it? Christ says: "This is how I will reward them. Whoever comes into the open and manifests himself as a true Christian will be loved by My Father, and I will also love him and manifest Myself to him." What does this mean? Did not Christ just tell His disciples that they would be in Him and He in them? Is not this already their lot by reason of their faith? Why does He say now that He will love them and manifest Himself to them? Has He not already done both? Yes, Christ has already begun and has laid the first stone. He suffered for me; He has His Gospel preached and has me baptized before I have asked for it or have known about Him. Then what does Christ mean here when He says that He will love those who love Him?

This is the answer: When a Christian has made the beginning and is now in Christ, believes in Him, and loves Him; when he begins to proclaim Him, to confess Him—then the devil attacks. And it seems to the Christian that God is up there in His heaven, not with us but entirely oblivious of us.

Therefore Christ consoles His suffering Christians here with the assurance that He will make His love apparent to them and will manifest Himself to them. As though He were to say: "Just continue with your love, and hold fast, even though it seems to you that I have gone as far from you as heaven is from the earth. For now you sometimes have an hour of adversity and do not feel Me in you.

"But do not let this dishearten you, for matters do not stand as you feel and think. I have another aid; I have other help for you, and more and more after that. Yes, I will come and manifest Myself in such a way that in your trials you will sense the sincere love which both My Father and I have for you."

Sermons on the Gospel of St. John (1537)
LW 24, 148–50

CHRISTIAN RIGHTEOUSNESS

O Lord, I am your sin; you are my righteousness. Therefore I triumph and am secure; for my sin cannot overpower your righteousness, nor can your righteousness let me be or remain a sinner. Blessed Lord God of mine, my Mercy and my Redeemer, in you only do I trust; never let me be ashamed. Amen.

What Luther Says, 3:1105, #3528

Monday

For in [the gospel] the righteousness of God is revealed through faith for faith; as it is written, "The one who is righteous will live by faith."   Romans 1:17

*H*e *is not righteous who does much, but he who, without work, believes much in Christ.* For the righteousness of God is not acquired by means of acts frequently repeated, as Aristotle taught, but it is imparted by faith, for "The one who through faith is righteous shall live" (Rom. 1:17), and "One believes with the heart and so is justified" (Rom. 10:10). Therefore I wish to have the words "without work" understood in the following manner: Not that the righteous person does nothing, but that the works do not make the person righteous; rather that the righteousness creates works. For grace and faith are infused without our works. After they have been imparted the works follow.

Thus Rom. 3:20 states, "No human being will be justified in His sight by works of the law," and, "For we hold that a person is justified by faith apart from works of law" (Rom. 3:28). In other words, works contribute nothing to justification. Therefore believers know that works which they do by such faith are not theirs but God's. For this reason they do not seek to become justified or glorified through them, but seek God. Their justification by faith in Christ is sufficient to them. Christ is their wisdom, righteousness, all things, as 1 Cor. 1:30 has it, that they themselves may be Christ's vessels and instruments.

"Heidelberg Disputation" (1518)
LW 31, 55–56

"And when he comes, he will prove the world wrong about sin and righteousness and judgment: . . . about righteousness, because I am going to the Father and you will see me no longer." John 16:8, 10

Tuesday

These words show exhaustively that Christ is not speaking here of outward, secular righteousness, which is important and necessary for this life. He is speaking here of a righteousness recognized by God, a righteousness far different from that acknowledged by the world. This righteousness He exalts far above all the works that can be done in this life and identifies it exclusively with Himself.

This is a peculiar righteousness. It is strange indeed that we are to be called righteous or to possess a righteousness which is really no work, no thought, in short, nothing whatever in us but is entirely outside us in Christ. Yet it becomes truly ours by reason of His grace and gift, and becomes our very own, as though we ourselves had achieved and earned it.

Reason, of course, cannot comprehend this way of speaking which says that our righteousness is something which involves nothing active or passive on our part. Yes, something in which I do not participate with my thoughts, perception, and senses; that nothing at all in me makes me pleasing to God and saves me; but that I leave myself and all human thoughts and ability out of account and cling to Christ, who sits up there at the right hand of God and whom I do not even see.

But in this verse I hear Christ say that my righteousness consists of His ascension into heaven. There my righteousness has been deposited, and there the devil will surely have to let it remain; for he will not make Christ a sinner or reprove or find fault with His righteousness.

Sermons on the Gospel of St. John (1537)
LW 24, 345–48

Wednesday

For we hold that a person is justified by faith apart from works prescribed by the law.   Romans 3:28

But the devil, that master of a thousand tricks, lays traps for us with marvelous cleverness. He leads some astray by getting them involved in open sins. Others, who think themselves righteous, he brings to a stop, makes them lukewarm as Rev. 3:14ff. A third group he seduces into superstitions and ascetic sects, so that, for example, they do not at all grow cold but feverishly engage in works, setting themselves apart from the others, whom they despise in their pride and disdain. A fourth class of people he urges on with ridiculous labor to the point where they try to be completely pure and holy, without any taint of sin.

He senses the weakness of each individual and attacks him in this area. And because these four classes of people are so fervent for righteousness, it is not easy to persuade them to the contrary. Thus he begins by helping them to achieve their goal, so that they become overanxious to rid themselves of every evil desire. When they cannot accomplish this, he causes them to become sad, dejected, wavering, hopeless, and unsettled in their consciences.

Then it only remains for us to stay in our sins and to cry in hope of the mercy of God that He would deliver us from them. Just as the patient who is too anxious to recover can surely have a serious relapse, we must also be healed gradually and for a while put up with certain weaknesses. For it is sufficient that our sin displeases us, even though we do not get entirely rid of it. For Christ carries all sins, if only they are displeasing to us, and thus they are no longer ours but His, and His righteousness in turn is ours.

Lectures on Romans (1515–16)
LW 25, 254

Christian Righteousness

I have been crucified with Christ; and it is no longer I who live, but it is Christ who lives in me. Galatians 2:19b-20a

Thursday

Paul shows how he is alive, and he states what Christian righteousness is. It is that righteousness by which Christ lives in us. Christ and my conscience must become one, so that nothing remains in my sight but Christ, crucified and risen. If I look only at myself, then I am done for. By paying attention to myself and considering what my condition is or should be, and what I am supposed to be doing, I lose sight of Christ.

This is an extremely common evil. In such conflicts of conscience, therefore, we must form the habit of leaving ourselves behind as well as the Law and all our works, which force us to pay attention to ourselves. We must turn our eyes completely to that bronze serpent, Christ nailed to the cross (John 3:14). We must declare with assurance that He is our Righteousness and Life. For the Christ on whom our gaze is fixed, in whom we exist, and who also lives in us, is the Victor and the Lord over the Law, sin, death, and every evil. In Him a sure comfort has been set forth for us, and victory has been granted.

Therefore, because Christ clings and dwells in us most intimately, we can say: "Christ is fixed and cemented to me and abides in me. The life that I now live, He lives in me. Indeed, Christ Himself is the life that I now live."

Lectures on Galatians (1535)
LW 26, 166–67

Christian Righteousness

Friday

Out of his anguish he shall see light; he shall find satisfaction through his knowledge. The righteous one, my servant, shall make many righteous, and he shall bear their iniquities.   Isaiah 53:11

A Christian cannot arrive at this knowledge by means of any laws, either moral or civil, but he must ascend to heaven by means of the Gospel. This is the vehicle by which the knowledge of God reaches us. There is no other plan or method of obtaining liberty than the knowledge of Christ. You must therefore note this new definition of righteousness. Righteousness is the knowledge of Christ, the One who bears all our sins.

The individual words *His knowledge* and *iniquities* must be pondered in supreme faith. They must be read and considered with the most watchful eyes, so that it is not simply any kind of knowledge or understanding but a knowledge that justifies. Thus you see this remarkable definition of righteousness through the knowledge of God. It sounds ridiculous to call righteousness a speculative knowledge. Therefore it is said in Jer. 9:24: "Let him who glories glory in this, that he understands and knows Me."

This knowledge, then, is the formal and substantial righteousness of the Christians, that is, faith in Christ, which I obtain through the Word. I receive the Word through the intellect, but to assent to that Word is the work of the Holy Spirit. It is not the work of reason, which always seeks its own kinds of righteousness. The Word, however, sets forth another righteousness through the consideration and the promises of Scripture, which cause this faith to be accounted for righteousness. This is our glory to know for certain that our righteousness is divine in that God does not impute our sins. Therefore our righteousness is nothing else than knowing God.

Lectures on Isaiah (1527–30)
LW 17, 229–30

GOD THE CREATOR

O God, we give thanks to you that in your kindness you have created us out of nothing into excellent beings with body and soul, intelligence, and five senses; that you provide for our daily needs out of nothing and have ordained us to be masters of earth, of fish, bird, and beast. Amen.

LW 43, 210 (paraphrase)

God the Creator

Monday

In the beginning when God created the heavens and the earth.   Genesis 1:1

The first article of the Apostles' Creed teaches that God is the Father, the creator of heaven and earth. What is this? What do these words mean? The meaning is that I should believe that I am God's creature, that he has given to me body, soul, good eyes, reason, a good wife, children, fields, meadows, pigs, and cows, and besides this, he has given to me the four elements, water, fire, air, and earth. Thus this article teaches that you do not have your life of yourself, not even a hair. I would not even have a pig's ear, if God had not created it for me. Everything that exists is comprehended in that little word "creator." Therefore, everything you have, however small it may be, remember this when you say "creator," even if you set great store by it. Do not let us think that we have created ourselves, as the proud princes do.

"Ten Sermons on the Catechism" (1528)
LW 51, 162–63

Then the LORD God formed man from the dust of the ground, and breathed into his nostrils the breath of life; and the man became a living being.   Genesis 2:7

Tuesday

I believe that he has given to me my life, my five senses, reason, spouse, and children. None of these do I have of myself. God is the "creator," that is, God has given everything, body and soul, including every member of the body. But if everything is the gift of God, then you owe it to him to serve him with all these things and praise and thank him, since he has given them and still preserves them. But, I ask you, how many are there in the world who understand this word "creator"? For nobody serves him. We sin against God with all our members, one after another, with wife, children, house, home.

In short, the first article of the Apostles' Creed teaches creation, the second redemption, the third sanctification. The creation, it teaches, means that I believe that God has given to me body, life, reason, and all that I possess. These things I have not of myself, that I may not become proud. I cannot either give them to myself or keep them by myself. But why has he given them to you and what do you think he gave them to you for? It is in order that you should praise him and thank him. There are many who say these words, "I believe in God the Father," but do not understand what these words mean.

"Ten Sermons on the Catechism" (1528)
LW 51, 163 64

Wednesday

For though the LORD is high, he regards the lowly.   Psalm 138:6a

Just as God in the beginning of creation made the world out of nothing, whence He is called the Creator and the Almighty, so His manner of working continues unchanged. Even now and to the end of the world, all His works are such that out of that which is nothing, worthless, despised, wretched, and dead, He makes that which is something, precious, honorable, blessed, and living. Therefore His eyes look only upon the lowly (Ps. 138:6). The eyes of the world and of men, on the contrary, look only above them and are lifted up with pride.

But to God alone belongs that sort of seeing that looks upon the lowly with their need and misery, and is near to all that are in the depths; as St. Peter says (1 Peter 5:5): "God opposes the proud but gives grace to the humble." And this is the source of believers' love and praise of God. For no one can praise God without first loving Him. No one can love Him unless He makes Himself known to them in the most lovable and intimate fashion. And He can make Himself known only through those words of His which He reveals in us, and which we feel and experience within ourselves. But where there is this experience, namely, that He is a God who looks upon the lowly and helps only the poor, despised, afflicted, miserable, forsaken, and those who are nothing, there a hearty love for Him is born.

Commentary on "The Magnificat" [Luke 1:46-55] (1521)
LW 21, 299–300

God the Creator

Then God spoke all these words: "I am the **Thursday**
LORD your God."   Exodus 20:1-2a

I take the risk of placing my confidence only in the one, invisible, inscrutable, and only God, who created heaven and earth and who alone is superior to all creation. Again, I am not terrified by all the wickedness of the devil and his cohorts because God is superior to them all.

I would believe in God not a bit less if everyone were to forsake me and persecute me. I would believe in God no less if I were poor, unintelligent, uneducated, despised, or lacking in everything. I believe no less though I am a sinner. For this manner of faith will of necessity rise over all that does or does not exist, over sin and virtue and all else, thus depending purely and completely upon God as the First Commandment enjoins me to do.

I do not ask for any sign from God to put him to the test. I trust in him steadfastly, no matter how long he may delay, prescribing neither a goal, nor a time, nor a measure, nor a way for God to respond to me, but leaving all to his divine will in a free, honest, and genuine faith.

If he is the Creator of heaven and earth and Lord over everything, who, then, could deprive me of anything, or work me harm (Rom. 8:31)? Yes, how can it be otherwise than that all things work for good for me (Rom. 8:28) if the God, whom all creation obeys and depends upon, is well intentioned toward me?

"Personal Prayer Book" (1522)
LW 43, 25–26

Friday

"Where, O death, is your victory? Where, O death, is your sting?"
1 Corinthians 15:55

When Isaac's throat was about to be cut, he thought: "Into Thy hands I commit my spirit (Ps. 31:5). I shall not die, but I shall live; and I shall return, because God will not lie. I am the son of the promise. Therefore I must beget children, even if heaven collapses." There was a great light of faith in that young man. He believed in God the Creator, who calls into existence the things that do not exist (Rom. 4:17), and commands the ashes that are not Isaac to be Isaac. For he who believes that God is the Creator, who makes all things out of nothing, must of necessity conclude that therefore God can raise the dead.

But all this has its source in the First of the Ten Commandments; for in it is contained the doctrine of faith and of the resurrection of the dead. "I, the almighty Creator of heaven and earth, am your God; that is, you must live the life I am living." If He were speaking these words to oxen, they would live forever. But they are said to us—to us, I say. He does not say to them: "You must eat chaff, wheat, and grass." No, He says: "I am your God."

Furthermore, to be God means to deliver from all evils that burden us, such as sin, hell, death; for in this manner the prophets regarded and interpreted these words. The heathen know God solely as the Creator; but in the First Commandment you will find Christ, life, victory over death, and the resurrection of the dead into eternal life, and finally the entire Old and New Testament. But only those who have the Holy Spirit and pay attention to what God says and does see this.

Lectures on Genesis (1539–40)
LW 4, 119–20

THE HOLY SPIRIT

Lord God, dear Father, who through your Holy Spirit did enlighten and teach the hearts of your faithful people: Grant to us that we may have right understanding through the same Spirit and at all times rejoice in his comfort and power; through your Son Jesus Christ our Lord. Amen.

LW 53, 135

Monday

"When the Spirit of truth comes, he will guide you into all the truth; for he will not speak on his own, but will speak whatever he hears, and he will declare to you the things that are to come."
John 16:13

Here Christ defines the Holy Spirit's office and points out what and about what He is to teach. He constantly keeps in mind the false spirits and preachers who boastfully claim to have the Holy Spirit and allege that what they say has emanated from the Holy Spirit. There are some who speak on their own authority; that is, they evolve their message from their own reasoning or religious zeal and judgment. The Holy Spirit is not to be that kind of preacher; for He will not speak on His own authority, and His message will not be a human dream and thought like that of the preachers who speak on their own authority of things which they have neither seen nor experienced.

"No," Christ says, "His message will have substance; it will be certain and absolute truth, for He will preach what He receives from the Father and from Me. And you will be able to recognize Him by the fact that He does not speak on His own authority—as the spirit of lies, the devil, and his mobs do—but will preach about what He will hear. Thus He will speak exclusively of Me and will glorify Me, so that the people will believe in Me."

In this way Christ sets bounds for the message of the Holy Spirit Himself. He is not to preach anything new or anything else than Christ and His Word.

Sermons on the Gospel of St. John (1537)
LW 24, 362–63

The Holy Spirit

*And because you are children, God has
sent the Spirit of his Son into our hearts.
Galatians 4:6a*

Tuesday

We must not doubt that the Holy Spirit dwells in us. We must be sure and acknowledge that we are a "temple of the Holy Spirit" (1 Cor. 6:19). For if someone experiences love toward the Word, and if he enjoys hearing, speaking, thinking and writing about Christ, he should know that this is not a work of human will or reason but a gift of the Holy Spirit.

And therefore we should believe that whatever we say, do, or think is pleasing to God, not on our account but on account of Christ. We are most certain that Christ is pleasing to God and that He is holy. To the extent that Christ is pleasing to God and that we cling to Him, we, too, are pleasing to God and holy. Although sin still clings to our flesh and we still fall every day, still grace is more abundant and more powerful than sin.

This inner assurance that we are in a state of grace and have the Holy Spirit is accompanied by the external signs I have mentioned: to enjoy hearing about Christ; to teach, give thanks, praise, and confess Him; to do one's duty according to one's calling; to help the needy and comfort the sorrowful. By these signs we are assured and confirmed that we are in a state of grace.

Lectures on Galatians (1535)
LW 26, 376, 378–79

Wednesday

... the Spirit of his Son ... crying, "Abba! Father!"   Galatians 4:6

It is a very great comfort that the Spirit of Christ, sent by God into our hearts, cries: "Abba! Father!" He helps us in our weakness and intercedes for us with sighs too deep for words. Anyone who truly believed this would not fall away in any affliction. But many things hinder this faith. Our heart was born in sin. Further, we have the innate evil in us that we doubt the favor of God toward us. We cannot believe with certainty that we are pleasing to Him. Besides, "our adversary, the devil, prowls around, issuing terrible roars" (1 Peter 5:8). He roars: "God is wrathful with you and will destroy you forever." We have nothing to strengthen and sustain us except the bare Word which sets Christ forth as the Victor over sin, death, and every evil. But it is effort and labor to cling firmly to this in the midst of trial and conflict. We do not see Christ, and in the trial our heart does not feel His presence and help. Then we feel the power of sin, the weakness of the flesh, and our doubt. We feel the fiery darts of the devil (Eph. 6:16).

Meanwhile, the Holy Spirit is helping us in our weakness and interceding for us. He merely utters the words of a cry and a sigh, which is "Oh, Father!" This is indeed a very short word, but it includes everything. It is as if one were to say: "Even though I am surrounded by anxieties and seem to be deserted and banished from Thy presence, nevertheless I am a child of God on account of Christ. I am beloved on account of the Beloved."

Therefore the term "Father," when spoken meaningfully in the heart, is an eloquence that Demosthenes, Cicero, and the most eloquent orators cannot attain.

Lectures on Galatians (1535)
LW 26, 380–81, 385

"And I will ask the Father, and he will give you another Advocate, to be with you forever." John 14:16

Thursday

Here we must note in what a friendly and comforting manner Christ speaks to all poor, saddened hearts and fearful, timid consciences. He shows us how we may truly recognize the Holy Spirit. We must learn to know and believe in the Holy Spirit as Christ describes Him. His is not a Spirit of anger and terror but a Spirit of grace and consolation. We are to know that the entire Deity reflects sheer comfort. The Father wants to comfort, for it is He who grants the Holy Spirit. The Son likewise, for He prays for this. And the Holy Spirit Himself is to be the Comforter [Advocate]. Here, therefore, there is no wrath, threat, or terror for Christians; there is only a friendly smile and sweet comfort in heaven and on earth.

But we forget. The devil is too powerful among us, the world is too strong, and we see so many obstacles and temptations before us that we forget and cannot comprehend the comfort God sends into our hearts. We feel only that which hurts us. It is so strong that it fills one's whole being and erases these words from one's mind.

Therefore Christians should rise above all fear and sadness and hear Christ: "I know this very well, and for this very reason I am telling you about it in advance. You should not be guided by such feelings or believe your own thoughts; you should believe My Word. For I will ask the Father and He will surely give you the Holy Spirit to comfort you. Then you can rest assured that I love you, the Father loves you, and the Holy Spirit, who is sent to you, loves you."

Sermons on the Gospel of St. John (1537)
LW 24, 103, 110–11, 114

Friday

When the Spirit of truth comes, he will guide you into all the truth.
John 16:13a

The Holy Spirit will teach the disciples and show them that everything Christ told them is the truth, for He is a Spirit who confirms the truth in one's heart and makes one sure of it.

The dear apostles surely found out, and their conduct toward their Lord Christ demonstrated adequately, how completely impossible—not only difficult—it is to retain faith in trials if one does not have the help of the Holy Spirit. In Christ's suffering and death they deserted Him ignominiously. They denied Him, and the faith in their hearts was practically extinguished by the thought inspired by the devil.

Thus true Christians always have discovered and still do that this faith which should hold firmly to the articles concerning Christ and His kingdom cannot be retained by human reason or power. The Holy Spirit Himself must accomplish this. It is a sure sign of the presence of the Holy Spirit and of His power when faith is preserved and is victorious in a real battle and trial.

All experience and the work itself show daily that in Christendom the Holy Spirit Himself must do everything that pertains to the real guidance of Christendom. For without Him we would not baptize or preach very long nor would we retain the name of Christ. In one hour the devil would have dispossessed us of everything and would have destroyed it.

Sermons on the Gospel of St. John (1537)
LW 24, 357, 359–60

THE TRINITY

Almighty eternal God, who has taught us to know and confess in true faith that you are one eternal God in three Persons of equal power and glory and to be worshiped as such: We pray that you would at all times keep us firm in this faith in spite of whatever opposition we may incur; who lives and reigns, world without end. Amen.

LW 53, 136

Monday

"All that the Father has is mine. For this reason I said that he will take what is mine and declare it to you."
John 16:15

These are all sublime words; for here Christ is speaking in His own way, not about the creatures but about the sublime and inscrutable essence in the Godhead.

Here the circle is completely closed, and all three—the Father, the Son, and the Holy Spirit—are embraced in one divine essence. Christ says: "From that which is Mine, which is the Father's, namely, the fact that I am one God with Him, the Holy Spirit also takes what He is and has. Therefore He is and has exactly what both the Father and I are and have. For if He takes and has what I have, it follows that He must be of the same nature and essence, since what I have for Myself and call My own cannot be ascribed to any creature." Now "to take what is Mine" does not mean to take or cut off a fraction or a particle from the Godhead, for the Godhead cannot be dismembered and divided; it is a perfect, complete, and indivisible essence. Accordingly, where there is a part, there the whole Godhead is certainly present.

Sermons on the Gospel of St. John (1537)
LW 24, 372–73

*And the Holy Spirit descended upon him
in bodily form like a dove. And a voice
came from heaven, "You are my Son, the
Beloved; with you I am well pleased."
Luke 3:22*

Tuesday

The heavens opened, the Father's voice was heard, and the Holy Spirit descended, not as a phantom but in the form and figure of a natural dove. Nor was the Father's voice an illusion when He pronounced these words from heaven: "This is My beloved Son; with Him I am well pleased." These were real, natural, human words. And this dove, in the form of which the Holy Spirit was seen, was real and natural. Nevertheless, it was the Holy Spirit.

All this was done in honor and praise of the Sacrament of Holy Baptism; for this is not a human institution but something sublime and holy. Eminent personages are involved in it: the Father who bestows and who speaks here; the Son, who receives and is baptized; the Holy Spirit, who hovers above and reveals Himself in the form of a dove. And the celestial choir of all the angels is present; these skip and dance for joy over this act. Furthermore, the entire heaven stands ajar.

But it is recorded here that all three persons of the Trinity, God the Father, God the Son, and God the Holy Spirit, together with all the elect angels, were present at Christ's Baptism, although invisibly, and heaven was open for the occasion. In fact, God the Father, Son, and Holy Spirit still attend our Baptism today.

Sermons on the Gospel of St. John (1537–40)
LW 22, 173–74

The Trinity

Wednesday

[The Holy Spirit] will speak whatever he hears. John 16:13c

Here it is relevant to state that Scripture calls our Lord Christ—according to His divine nature—a "Word" (John 1:1) which the Father speaks with and in Himself. Thus this Word has a true, divine nature from the Father. It is not a word spoken by the Father as a physical, natural word spoken by a human being is a voice or a breath that does not remain within but comes out and remains outside. No, this Word remains in the Father forever. Thus these are two distinct Persons: He who speaks and the Word that is spoken, that is, the Father and the Son.

Here, however, we find the third Person following these two, namely, the One who hears both the Speaker and the spoken Word. For there must also be a listener where a speaker and a word are found. But all this speaking, being spoken, and listening takes place within the divine nature and also remains there, where no creature is or can be. All three—Speaker, Word, and Listener—must be God Himself. All three must be coeternal and in a single undivided majesty. For there is no difference or inequality in the divine essence, neither a beginning nor an end. Therefore, one cannot say that the Listener is something outside God, or that there was a time when He began to be a Listener. But just as the Father is a Speaker from eternity, and just as the Son is spoken from eternity, so the Holy Spirit is the Listener from eternity.

Sermons on the Gospel of St. John (1537)
LW 24, 364–65

And God said, "Let the waters bring forth swarms of living creatures . . ." So God created the great sea monsters . . . And God saw that it was good.   Genesis 1:20-21

Thursday

Here we must deal also with what the holy fathers, and Augustine in particular, have noted, namely, that Moses employs these three words—"God said," "He made [created]," "He saw"—as if in this manner he wanted to point to the three Persons of the Divine Majesty. By the term "He said" the Father is denoted. He begets the Word in eternity and in time establishes this world through that Word. Therefore they have attributed the verb "made" to the Person of the Son. The Son has in Himself not only the image of the Divine Majesty but also the image of all created things. Therefore He bestows existence on things. Just as the objects are spoken by the Father, so all things have their existence through the Son and the Word of the Father. To these, however, is joined the Third Person, the Holy Spirit, who "sees" the created things and approves them.

Further, according to St. Hilary, when the text says: "And God saw that it was very good," it refers to the preservation itself, because the creature could not continue in existence unless the Holy Spirit delighted in it and preserved the work through this delight of God in His work. God did not create things with the idea of abandoning them after they had been created, but He loves them and expresses His approval of them. Therefore He is together with them. He sets in motion, He moves, and He preserves each according to its own manner.

Lectures on Genesis (1535–36)
LW 1, 49–51

Friday

The king will desire your beauty. Since he is your lord, bow to him.   Psalm 45:11

If we cannot grasp how God is one and three persons, we should leave that up to Him. We should only incline our ear. He Himself says that our King [Jesus Christ] is God, and He commands us to adore Him. If you reject this King in the foolish superstition that you might break the First Commandment, then you have rejected the entire and true God, as the Arians [fourth century heretics] did.

If they object: "Then you make many gods," I reply: "I do not make another or many gods, but I say that Father, Son, and Holy Spirit are one and the same God. There is a unity of substance and one Essence though there are three Persons. I do not want to have many gods, because many gods contend among themselves. Nor can there be many gods. But here is unity. If I do not understand how the Persons are differentiated, it is enough for me that Holy Scriptures say this and call Father, Son, and Holy Spirit by name (Matt. 28:19).

"If I could grasp this with my reason or senses, what need would there be for faith? Or what use is Scripture revealed by God through the Holy Spirit? If I believe nothing but what I can comprehend by my reason, I must reject Baptism, the Sacrament of the Altar, the Word, grace, original sin, and everything. Reason understands none of these things."

Commentary on "Psalm 45" (1532)
LW 12, 286–88

THE CHURCH

Almighty everlasting God, who through your Holy Spirit sanctifies and rules the whole church: Hear our prayer and graciously grant that it with all its members, by your grace, may serve you in true faith; through Jesus Christ your Son our Lord. Amen.

LW 53, 141

The Church

Monday

This is the gate of the LORD; the righteous shall enter through it.   Psalm 118:20

Hypocrites, scoundrels, and sinners entered the gate of that temple; but only the righteous and the saints enter this gate of the Lord in order to serve Him. For none can enter the Christian congregation or be members of Christendom unless they are believers, that is righteous and holy, as the article of the Creed says: "I believe in the Holy Christian Church."

Therefore I hope that by this time almost everybody knows that those who pride themselves on being Christians must also take pride in being holy and righteous. Since Christendom is holy, Christians must also be righteous and holy, or they are not Christians. All Scripture calls Christians holy and righteous, as does this verse. This is not boastfulness. It is a necessary confession and an article of faith.

We must realize that in our persons as children of Adam we are damned sinners, without any righteousness or holiness of our own. However, since we are baptized and believe in Christ, we are holy and righteous in Christ and with Christ. He has taken our sin from us and has graced, clothed, and adorned us with His holiness. Therefore any who hesitate to boast and confess that they are holy and righteous, are actually saying: "I am not baptized. I am not a Christian. I do not believe that Christ died for me. I do not believe a word of what God has declared of Christ and all Scripture testified."

But we are assured that the whole Christian Church is holy, not by itself or by its own work but in Christ and through Christ's holiness, as St. Paul says: "He has cleansed her by the washing of water with the Word" (Eph. 5:26).

Commentary on "Psalm 118" (1530)
LW 14, 92–93

At your right hand stands the queen in gold of Ophir.   Psalm 45:9b

The remission of sins and the whole treasure of divine mercy cannot be more excellently painted or described than that the church should be called the bride of Christ, His queen. It follows from this picture that the bride has everything that is Christ's. What does Christ have? Eternal righteousness, wisdom, power, truth, life, joy, grace. This is a most beautiful transformation, that the church, miserable in the eyes of men, should be so richly adorned in the eyes of God.

Therefore these are great and incomparable words, to hear that Jesus Christ is the Bridegroom and the church is the bride. In fact, they are heavenly and infinite words. They cannot be grasped by the heart of any person nor ever learned completely. To those who brag that they know these things you could say that they have merely heard some echo of this teaching but are ignorant of the matter itself.

I am saying this as an encouragement to you to ponder these words of the Holy Spirit. He speaks them for our comfort, in order that we may learn to extend them richly. No one can hear too much about this or grasp Christ too firmly. Grasp as much as you can, and you will still see that you are lacking something and that you cannot trust as much in the Bridegroom as He requires and we need. Satan, sin, flesh, blood, and our reason are still present. They oppose your grasping Him. And yet if you grasp Him, whether little or much, you have the Bridegroom, and through Him life and salvation. You are part of the church, His bride and queen.

Commentary on "Psalm 45" (1532)
LW 12, 261–63

The Church

Wednesday

Let us consider how to provoke one another to love and good deeds.
Hebrews 10:24

The church of this time has been gathered from the diverse believers of the world. Very many who are weak, impotent, imperfect, and sinful have been intermingled. But human nature is constituted in such a way that it prefers to deal with those who are good and perfect to dealing with those who are imperfect and difficult. Because of this sin, those who are weaker cause those who are more perfect to be haughty, to despise, to judge, etc. On the other hand, those who are more perfect cause those who are weaker to envy and disparage. Therefore the apostles strove with all their might to counter this evil, lest schisms and heresies arise in the church.

These, of course, are prevented only by mutual love. Furthermore, the love that is shown to equals or betters is (as one sees everywhere) either no love at all, or it is not Christian, as Matt. 5:43-47 states: "You have heard that it was said to those of old: 'You shall love your friend and hate your enemy.' But I say to you: 'Love your enemies, do good to those who hate you, pray for those who persecute and slander you. For if you love only those who love you, what reward will you have? Do not even the tax collectors do this?'"

This, therefore, is the Christian love that is shown to those who are contemptible and unworthy of love. This, in fact, is the kindness that is bestowed on those who are evil and ungrateful. For this is what Christ and God did for us; and we, too, are commanded to love as He did.

"Lectures on Hebrews" (1517–18)
LW 29, 226–27

Thursday

He replied, "Do not be afraid, for there are more with us than there are with them."   2 Kings 6:16

This is the church of the saints, the new creation of God, our brothers and our friends, in whom we see nothing but blessing and nothing but consolation, though not always with the eyes of the flesh but with the eyes of the spirit. Whose heart will not be lifted up, even in the midst of great evils, when he believes the very truth, namely, that the blessings of all the saints are his blessings, and his evil is also theirs?

Therefore, when we feel pain, when we suffer, when we die, let us turn to this thought, firmly believing and certain that it is not we alone, but Christ and the church who are in pain and are suffering and dying with us. Christ does not want us to be alone on the road of death, from which all people shrink. Indeed, we set out upon the road of suffering and death accompanied by the entire church. Actually, the church bears it more bravely than we do. Thus we can truthfully apply to ourselves the words Elisha spoke to his fearful servants, "Fear not, for those who are with us are more numerous than those with them. And Elisha prayed and said, 'Lord open the eyes of the young man that he may see.' And the Lord opened his eyes and he saw. And behold, the mountain was full of horses and chariots of fire around Elisha" (2 Kings 6:16-17).

All that remains for us now is to pray that our eyes, that is the eyes of our faith, may be opened that we may see the church around us.

"Fourteen Consolations" (1520)
LW 42, 160–61, 163

The Church

Friday

I believe in ... the holy Christian Church, the communion of saints. (from The Apostles' Creed)

The Christian church is your mother, who gives birth to you and bears you through the Word. And this is done by the Holy Spirit who bears witness concerning Christ.

When you hear the word "church," understand that it means group or congregation; that is, a holy, Christian group, assembly or, in German, the holy, common church, and it is a word which should not be called "communion," but rather "a congregation." "Christian church" and "congregation of saints" are one and the same thing.

In other words: I believe that there is a holy group and a congregation made up only of saints. And you too are in this church; the Holy Spirit leads you into it through the preaching of the gospel. Through the Christian church, that is, through its ministry, you were sanctified; for the Holy Spirit uses its ministry in order to sanctify you. Otherwise you would never know and hear Christ.

Then, in this Christian church, you have "the forgiveness of sins." This term includes baptism, consolation upon a deathbed, the sacrament of the altar, absolution, and all the comforting passages of the gospel. In this term are included all the ministrations through which the church forgives sins, especially where the gospel, not laws or traditions, is preached. Outside of this church and these sacraments and ministrations there is no sanctification.

"Ten Sermons on the Catechism" (1528)
LW 51, 166–67

SUMMER

BAPTISM

The almighty God and Father of our Lord Jesus Christ, who has regenerated you through water and the Holy Spirit and has forgiven you all your sin, strengthen you with his grace to life everlasting. Amen.

LW 53, 109

Baptism

Monday

And he said to them, "Go into all the world and proclaim the good news to the whole creation. The one who believes and is baptized will be saved; but the one who does not believe will be condemned."
Mark 16:15-16

This is a strict command; if people want to be saved, let them be baptized; otherwise they are in God's disfavor. Therefore, these words are in the first place a strict, earnest divine command. Hence you cannot hold the opinion that baptism is a human invention or any kind of command or thing, such as putting a wreath on one's head— it is God's command. Consequently, you must esteem baptism as something high, glorious, and excellent; for here there is a divine word and command, which institutes and confirms baptism.

Certainly when the devil sees baptism and hears the Word sounding, to him it is like a bright sun and he will not stay there, and when a person is baptized for the sake of the Word of God, which is in it, there is a veritable oven glow. Do you think it was a joke that the heavens were opened at Christ's baptism? (Matt. 3:16). Say, therefore, that baptism is water and God's Word comprehended in one. Take the Word away and it is the same water with which the maid waters the cow; but with the Word, it is a living, holy, divine water. Those who consider the words: "will be saved" (Mark 16:16) will find salvation; for with his words, "will be saved," Christ puts salvation into baptism. Therefore it is impossible that this should be simple water when through it salvation, forgiveness of sins, and redemption from death and the devil is given.

"Ten Sermons on the Catechism" (1528)
LW 51, 183–84

And John testified, "I saw the Spirit descending from heaven like a dove, and it remained on him." John 1:32

Tuesday

Since Baptism is a divine act in which God Himself participates and since it is attended by the three exalted Persons of the Godhead, it must be prized and honored. One must agree that Baptism was not invented by any mortal but was instituted by God. It is not plain water but has God's Word in it and with it; and this transforms such water into a soul bath and into a bath of rejuvenation.

Thus we have seen from this text what a glorious thing Baptism is and that we are to esteem it highly. For John hears the voice of the Father proclaiming the Son. The Son, in human form, is standing in the Jordan. The Holy Spirit descends in the form of a dove. Consequently, exalted Persons are in attendance. From this you may gather that Baptism is not the work of mortals but of God, the Heavenly Father, whose voice is heard from above, saying: "This is My beloved Son" [Matt. 3:17]. It is also the work of God the Holy Spirit, who hovers over the scene in the form of a dove; and also the work of God the Son, who accepts the Baptism of John on His person. And we have the same glorious company at our own Baptism, which means that it is not the work of mortals but solely of God, the sublime Majesty, of the three Persons in the Godhead, who are one in essence, power, and majesty.

Sermons on the Gospel of St. John (1537–40)
LW 22, 174, 180–81

Of course, we are well aware that Baptism is natural water. But

Baptism

Wednesday

Jesus answered him, "Very truly, I tell you, no one can see the kingdom of God without being born from above."
John 3:3

Christ discusses these matters at length with Nicodemus, but Nicodemus cannot understand them.

Of course, we are well aware that Baptism is natural water. But after the Holy Spirit is added to it, we have more than mere water. It becomes a veritable bath of rejuvenation, a living bath which washes and purges us of sin and death, which cleanses us of all sin.

Christ wants to say: "You are not yet born anew. But I have come to bring you a new way of being born again, namely, a rebirth by water and the Holy Spirit, and to proclaim to you the necessity of this rebirth. I bring you a washing of regeneration which gives you a new birth and transforms you into a new person."

Therefore Christ says to Nicodemus here: "Come to Me and be baptized with water and the Holy Spirit, a Baptism that will give you a new birth and transform you into a new person, that will cause a regeneration or a renewal of your being." For the Holy Spirit works faith in us, and through this faith we regain the image of God which we lost in Paradise. If we are baptized and believe that Christ died for us, we will increase from day to day in faith as well as in the fruits and good works of the Holy Spirit. "Whoever would be saved, let them accept My message; for now is the time for My proclamation," Christ says.

Sermons on the Gospel of St. John (1537–40)
LW 22, 282–86

Happy are those whose transgression is forgiven, whose sin is covered.
Psalm 32:1

Thursday

We must humbly admit, "I know full well that I cannot do a single thing that is pure. But I am baptized, and through my baptism God, who cannot lie, has bound himself in a covenant with me. He will not count my sin against me, but will slay it and blot it out."

So, then, we understand that the innocence which is ours by baptism is so called simply and solely because of the mercy of God. For he has begun this work in us, he bears patiently with our sin, and he regards us as if we were sinless. This also explains why Christians are called in the Scriptures the children of mercy, a people of grace, and people of God's good will.

Baptism is indeed that great a thing, that if you turn again from sins and appeal to the covenant of baptism, your sins are forgiven. But watch out, if you thus wickedly and wantonly sin and go presuming on God's grace, that the judgment does not lay hold upon you and anticipate your turning back.

Let us therefore walk with fear, that with a firm faith we may hold fast to the riches of God's grace and joyfully give thanks to his mercy forever and ever. Amen.

Treatise on "The Holy and Blessed Sacrament of Baptism" (1519)
LW 35, 36, 43

Baptism

Friday

They shall be mine, says the LORD of hosts, my special possession on the day when I act, and I will spare them as parents spare their children who serve them.   Malachi 3:17

If, then, the holy sacrament of baptism is a matter so great, gracious, and full of comfort, we should diligently see to it that we ceaselessly, joyfully, and from the heart thank, praise, and honor God for it. For I fear that by our thanklessness we have deserved our blindness and become unworthy of recognizing such grace. The whole world was, and still is, full of baptism and the grace of God. But we have been led astray into our own anxious works, and then into indulgences and other similar false comforts. We have thought that we are not to trust God until we are righteous and have made satisfaction for our sin, as though we would buy God's grace from him or pay him for it.

In truth, those who do not see in God's grace how it bears with them as sinners and will make them blessed, they who look forward only to God's judgment, will never be joyful in God, and can neither love nor praise him. But if we hear and firmly believe that in the covenant of baptism God receives us sinners, spares us, and makes us pure from day to day, then our heart must be joyful, and love and praise God.

Treatise on "The Holy and Blessed Sacrament of Baptism" (1519)
LW 35, 42

THE LORD'S SUPPER

We give thanks to you, Almighty God, that you have refreshed us with this salutary gift; and we beseech you in your mercy to strengthen us through the same gift in faith toward you, and in fervent love among us all; for the sake of Jesus Christ our Lord. Amen.

LW 53, 138

Monday

The LORD Jesus on the night when he was betrayed took a loaf of bread, and when he had given thanks, he broke it and said, "This is my body that is for you. Do this in remembrance of me."
1 Corinthians 11:23b-24

Mark well the phrase "in remembrance of me," for with it Christ wants to induce and encourage you, out of love and gratitude to him and in praise and honor of his suffering, to participate in the sacrament gladly or at least gladly to be present for its observance. Also the words "for you" are to be diligently noted in this connection, when he says: "My body which is for you." The two words "my" and "you" are indeed mighty words which should fairly impel you gladly to walk over a hundred thousand miles for this sacrament. For if you would consider who it is who speaks "my," and who says, "Do this in remembrance of me," you would discover that it is your dear Lord Christ Jesus, God's Son, who shed his blood and died for you. He desires no more of you with this word "my" than that you might recognize and believe the same, that you acknowledge it, and thank him that he went to such great pains to achieve it.

What heart can comprehend with increasing adequacy what a benefit and grace it is that one is redeemed from death and the devil, from sins and all evil, and is righteous, alive, and blessed without one's merit and help, only through the blood and dying of the Son of God?

"Admonition Concerning the Sacrament of the Body
and Blood of Our Lord" (1530)
LW 38, 125

Examine yourselves, and only then eat of the bread and drink of the cup.
1 Corinthians 11:28

Tuesday

Dear fellow, you must not look at yourself, how worthy or unworthy you are, but at your need—your need of the grace of Christ. If you see and feel your need, you are worthy and sufficiently prepared, for he has not instituted the sacrament to act as a poison and to harm us, but to grant comfort and salvation.

Therefore, observe what a fine sacrament this is when you simultaneously give thanks for previous grace and pray for future gifts of grace. Who can keep on thanking and praying enough? Consequently, there is no reason for becoming sluggish and lazy; there is only ardent, fervent inducement so that we should readily receive the sacrament with delight and joy. Oh, if the dear prophets and patriarchs had only seen and heard of such a sacrament, how glad and desirous of it they would have been. How they would have been amazed that we should be such blessed people as compared with them! On the other hand, how it would have hurt them if they would have seen that we despise it so disgracefully.

Not that I would want to force or coerce a person to go to the sacrament, for God does not want to have a coerced servant. However, I would like to give this admonition so that all Christians, on the basis of their own devotion, might constrain and obligate himself to obtain such a valued, precious treasure for the soul.

"Admonition Concerning the Sacrament of the Body
and Blood of Our Lord" (1530)
LW 38, 132–33, 135

The Lord's Supper

Wednesday

The cup of blessing that we bless, is it not a sharing in the blood of Christ? The bread that we break, is it not a sharing in the body of Christ? Because there is one bread, we who are many are one body, for we all partake of the one bread.
1 Corinthians 10:16-17

The sacrament has no blessing and significance unless love grows daily and so changes a person that that person is made one with all others. To signify this fellowship, God has appointed such signs of this sacrament as in every way serve this purpose and by their very form stimulate and motivate us to this fellowship. For just as the bread is made out of many grains ground and mixed together, and out of the bodies of the many grains there comes the body of one bread, in which each grain loses its form and body and takes upon itself the common body of the bread; and just as the drops of wine, in losing their own form, become the body of one common wine and drink— so it is and should be with us, if we use this sacrament properly.

Christ with all saints, by his love, takes upon himself our form (Phil. 2:7), fights with us against sin, death, and all evil. This enkindles in us such love that we take on his form, rely upon his righteousness, life, and blessedness. And through the interchange of his blessings and our misfortunes, we become one loaf, one bread, one body, one drink, and have all things in common. O this is a great sacrament, says St. Paul, that Christ and the church are one flesh and bone.

Treatise on "The Blessed Sacrament of the Holy and True Body of Christ, and the Brotherhoods" (1519)
LW 35, 58

He has gained renown by his wonderful deeds; the LORD is gracious and merciful. Psalm 111:4

Thursday

Now, if you are afraid to go to the Sacrament, and your conscience frightens you, as if you were unworthy, put this verse into your heart and on your lips. Then you must hear and feel how sincerely Christ calls and invites you. He is here and is waiting for you with hands and heart wide open, for you to take and receive grace and mercy. He does not want you to flee and shy away from Him but to flee to Him and with full confidence go to Him. Here He is called nothing but this: *the gracious and merciful Lord.* Do not give Him a different name in your heart or make Him anything else in your conscience. You would do Him an injustice and a great wrong, and yourself the greatest harm.

Whoever is inclined to put pictures on the altar ought to have the Lord's Supper of Christ painted, with these two verses written around it in golden letters: "The gracious and merciful Lord has instituted a remembrance of His wonderful works." Then they would stand before our eyes for our heart to contemplate them, and even our eyes, in reading would have to thank and praise God.

Thus this verse expresses not merely the fruit and benefit of the Sacrament—that it is a gracious and merciful institution in which one should seek and find grace and mercy—but it also exalts the remembrance of Christ.

Commentary on "Psalm 111" (1530)
LW 13, 374–75

Friday

For all who eat and drink without discerning the body, eat and drink judgment against themselves.
1 Corinthians 11:29

It is very necessary here that your hearts and consciences be well instructed and that you make a big distinction between outward reception and inner and spiritual reception. Bodily and outward reception is that in which a person receives with the mouth the body of Christ and his blood, and doubtless anyone can receive the sacrament in this way, without faith and love. But this does not make one a Christian, for if it did, even a mouse would be a Christian, for it, too, can eat the bread and perchance even drink out of the cup. It is such a simple thing to do. But the true, inner spiritual reception is a very different thing, for it consists in the right use of the sacrament and its fruits.

I would say in the first place that this reception occurs in faith and is inward and will have Christ. Without faith outward reception is nothing. Christianity consists solely in faith, and no outward work must be attached to it.

But faith is a firm trust that Christ, the Son of God, stands in our place and has taken all our sins upon his shoulders and that he is the eternal satisfaction for our sin and reconciles us with God the Father. Those who have this faith are the very ones who take their rightful place at this sacrament, and neither devil nor hell nor sin can harm them.

"Eight Sermons at Wittenberg" (1522)
LW 51, 92

GOD'S WORD

O heavenly Father, since no one likes your will and since we are too weak to have our will and our old Adam mortified, we pray that you will feed us, strengthen and comfort us with your holy Word, and grant us your grace that the heavenly bread Jesus Christ, may be preached and heard in all the world, that we may know it in our hearts, and so that all harmful, heretical, erroneous, and human doctrine may cease and only your Word, which is truly our living bread, be distributed. Amen.

LW 42, 61

Monday

Then he began to speak, and taught them,
saying: "Blessed are the poor in spirit, for
theirs is the kingdom of heaven."
Matthew 5:2-3

This is a fine, sweet, and friendly beginning for Christ's instruction and preaching. He does not come like Moses or a teacher of the Law, with demands, threats, and terrors, but in a very friendly way, with enticements, allurements, and pleasant promises. In fact, if it were not for this report which has preserved for us the first dear words that the Lord Christ preached, curiosity would drive and impel everyone to run all the way to Jerusalem just to hear one word of it. And all people would proudly boast that they had heard or read the very word that the Lord Christ had preached. That is exactly how it would really be if we had none of this in written form, even though there might be a great deal written by others. Everyone would say: "Yes, I hear what St. Paul and His other apostles have taught, but I would much rather hear what He Himself spoke and preached."

But now since it is so common that everyone has it written in a book and can read it every day, no one thinks of it as anything special or precious. Yes, we grow sated and neglect it, as if it had been spoken by some shoemaker rather than the High Majesty of heaven. Therefore it is in punishment for our ingratitude and neglect that we get so little out of it and never feel nor taste what a treasure, power, and might there is in the words of Christ. But whoever has the grace to recognize it as the Word of God rather than the word of mortals, will also think of it more highly and dearly, and will never grow sick and tired of it.

Commentary on "The Sermon on the Mount" (1532)
LW 21, 10

You grumbled in your tents and said, "It is because the LORD hates us that he has brought us out of the land of Egypt, to hand us over to the Amorites to destroy us."   Deuteronomy 1:27

Tuesday

See what a great disaster that tiny first beginning of doubt and the turning to trust in human prudence finally brings with it. Having now totally forgotten all the promises and wonders of God and being absorbed only in their own plans, the Children of Israel become worthy of listening to false messengers and preachers. Those messengers proclaim, and these people believe, greater things than the facts warrant. Instead of giving assent to the true Word of God, they give in to the lies of men.

Unbelief runs riot because the Word of God is lost, and in vain do Joshua and Caleb try to impress upon them the promise and truth of God [Numbers 14:6-9]. Godlessness conquers, and the lie wins out; truth lies prostrate. This is the fruit of human prudence and power in matters that belong to God. Finally they come to blasphemy. "The Lord hates us," they say.

This is the gratitude for the many miracles shown them. How could one ever overstate this most evil example of unbelief? After believers have begun to mistrust God, whom they previously considered propitious, they make God an object of their hatred. For when His Word is changed, He Himself is changed; for He Himself is in His Word.

Note, therefore, that godlessness makes dangers more and greater than they are, but it cares nothing for the Word of God. On the other hand, godliness regards all dangers, even the greatest, as nothing and the Word of God as the power of God (Rom. 1:16).

Lectures on Deuteronomy (1523–25)
LW 9, 22

Wednesday

In the beginning was the Word, and the Word was with God, and the Word was God.   John 1:1

The apostle affirmed clearly and distinctly that God is a Word and that this Word is with God, yes, is God Himself. We must realize that this Word *in* God is entirely different from my word or yours. For we, too, have a word, especially a "word of the heart," as the holy fathers call it. When, for example, we think about something and diligently investigate it, we have words; we carry on a conversation with ourselves.

Now a word is not merely the utterance of the mouth; rather it is the thought of the heart. Without this thought the external word is not spoken; or if it is spoken, it has substance only when the word of the mouth is in accord with the word of the heart. Thus God, too, from all eternity has a Word, a speech, a thought, or a conversation with Himself in His divine heart, unknown to angels and mortals. This is called His Word. From eternity He was within God's paternal heart, and through Him God resolved to create heaven and earth. But no one was aware of such a resolve until the Word became flesh and proclaimed this to us. This we shall see later in the words (John 1:18): "The Son, who is in the bosom of the Father, has revealed it to us."

Sermons on the Gospel of St. John (1537–40)
LW 22, 7–9

God's Word

Take the . . . sword of the Spirit, which is the word of God. Ephesians 6:17

Thursday

Since we are in the midst of enemies, we do not have a more effective power of overcoming and ruling over them than the rod of the strength of Christ, that is, the Gospel. But however often the spirit is tempted by whatever lust, if it recalls to mind the Word of God, it feels it, since His Word is effective and does not enter the memory without strength, as experience teaches. Hence, if you are tempted by anger and impatience, if you think of this or something similar: "By endurance you will gain what is yours" (Luke 21:19) or "Servants are not greater than their master" (John 13:16), you will immediately feel that the passion has abated.

Hence in Isa. 50:4 Christ and the church glory over this and say: "The Lord has given me a learned tongue, that I may know how to uphold by word him that is weary"; and Rom. 15:4: "that through patience and comfort of the Scriptures we might have hope." Therefore he rightly says, "the Lord will send forth out of Zion," (Ps. 110:2) that is, out of the watchtower of our memory, leading forth out of forgetfulness into the understanding that must now be considered: Then you will be able to rule. However, this is so if those who are tempted are people of good will. To those who desire to live piously and suffer persecution (2 Tim. 3:12), this is the rod of strength, the sword of the Spirit.

First Lectures on The Psalms II (1513–15)
LW 11, 365

Friday

Preach the Word; be prepared in season and out of season; correct, rebuke and encourage—with great patience and careful instruction.
2 Timothy 4:2 (NIV)

I preach the gospel of Christ, and with my bodily voice I bring Christ into your heart, so that you may form him within yourself. If now you truly believe, so that your heart lays hold of the word and holds fast within it that voice, tell me, what have you in your heart? You must answer that you have the true Christ, not that he sits in there, as one sits on a chair, but as he is at the right hand of the Father. How that comes about you cannot know, but your heart truly feels his presence, and through the experience of faith you know for a certainty that he is there.

Now I can accomplish this again, that the one Christ enters into so many hearts through the voice, and that each person who hears the sermon and accepts it takes the whole Christ into his heart. For Christ does not permit himself to be divided into parts; yet he is distributed whole among all the faithful, so that one heart receives no less, and a thousand hearts no more, than the one Christ. This we must ever confess, and it is a daily miracle. Indeed, it is as great a miracle as here in the sacrament.

Treatise on "The Sacrament of the Body and Blood of Christ—Against the Fanatics" (1526)
LW 36, 340

PRAYER

O Heavenly Father, dear God, I am a poor unworthy sinner. I do not deserve to raise my eyes or hands toward you or to pray. But because you have commanded us all to pray and have promised to hear us, and through your dear Son Jesus Christ have taught us both how and what to pray, I come to you in obedience to your word, trusting in your gracious promise. I pray in the name of my Lord Jesus Christ. Amen.

LW 43, 194

Monday

*And Abraham said to God, "O that
Ishmael might live in your sight!" God
said, "No, but your wife Sarah shall bear
you a son, and you shall name him Isaac."
Genesis 17:18-19a*

One may observe here that God always grants more than we are
able to ask for or to understand. Accordingly, one should learn that
those who want to pray properly should accustom themselves to pray
with confidence and not to be deterred either by the greatness of the
things to be granted or by the unworthiness of their praying.

There is a very beautiful example in Monica, the mother of
Augustine [a fifth century bishop], who prayed for her son and asked
for nothing else than that he be delivered from the foolish ideas of
the Manichaeans and be baptized. Like an anxious mother, she also
considered betrothing a girl to him if in this way he might be converted.

But the more she prayed, the more unyielding and stubborn her
son became. But when the time had come for the anxious prayer to
be heard (for God is wont to delay His help), Augustine is not only
converted and baptized. He devotes himself completely to the study
of theology and becomes a teacher who shines in the church up to
this day and teaches and instructs it.

Monica had never asked for this. She would have been satisfied
to have her son delivered from his error and become a Christian. But
God wants to give greater things than we are able to ask for, provided
that we do not tire of praying.

Lectures on Genesis (1538)
LW 3, 157–60

She never left the temple but worshiped there with fasting and prayer night and day.   Luke 2:37b

Tuesday

Anna prayed day and night, and this surely indicates, too, that she was awake. But this must not be understood to mean that she prayed and fasted day and night, without interruption. Naturally, she also had to eat, drink, sleep, and rest. The meaning is rather that such works made up her life; these were the things she did day and night. What a person does during the day and night must not therefore be understood to refer to the whole day and the whole night.

"Prayer," here is understood to be not only oral prayer, but everything the soul does in God's word—hearing, speaking, composing, meditating, and the like. Quite a few psalms are recited as prayers and yet in them scarcely three verses offer petitions. The other verses say and teach something; they punish sin, they invite us to talk with God, with ourselves, and with people. Such works were the service rendered to God by all the saints of old.

But our prayer today occurs solely in the babbling of words. Nobody thinks seriously to ask or receive something from God; rather prayer is undertaken as an obligation and one leaves it at that. They give no thought at all to the fact that they should serve God with prayer, that is, that they should pray for the common needs of Christendom. If they were to serve God and their neighbor with their praying they would not think of the number of psalms and individual words they had prayed. Rather they would think about how seriously they were seeking in these things God's honor and their neighbor's salvation, which is the true service of God. That would be true prayer and divine service like that of Anna.

Sermon on "The Gospel for the Sunday after Christmas,
Luke 2[:33-40]" (1522)
LW 52, 139–40

Week Four • Summer • 197

Wednesday

Before they call I will answer.
Isaiah 65:24a

This is a very lovely promise: "I will answer before they call." This promise is extremely necessary for strengthening our hearts and inciting them to pray. In the presence of God our prayers are regarded in such a way that they are answered before we call. The prayer of the righteous man is answered before it is finished. Before the prayer begins to formulate, while he is still speaking in general, it is answered as in Psalm 21:2: "Thou hast given him his heart's desire."

So Bernard [twelfth century French monk and mystic] says to his brothers: "Do not despise prayers, and know that as soon as you will have raised your voices, they are written in heaven, and it will come to pass and it will be given you. If it is not given, then it is not good for you, and God will give you something in its place that is better and more useful." This statement of Bernard comes from the Holy Spirit.

Thus if I pray, I am anticipating a great thing in my prayer. And our prayer pleases God; He requires it and delights in it. He promises, commands and shapes it. God cannot get enough of the prayers of the godly. Therefore the prayer of the godly is likened to the most attractive odor which one cannot smell enough. Then He says: "I will hear."

Lectures on Isaiah (1527–30)
LW 17, 392–93

Thursday

And God, who searches the heart, knows what is the mind of the Spirit, because the Spirit intercedes for the saints according to the will of God. Romans 8:27

Christian people are precious in God's sight and their prayer is powerful and great, for they have been sanctified by Christ's blood and anointed with the Spirit of God. Whatever they sincerely pray for, especially in the unexpressed yearning of their hearts, becomes a great, unbearable cry in God's ears. God must listen, as he did to Moses (Exod. 14:15). There God said, "Why do you cry to me?" even though Moses couldn't whisper, so great was his anxiety and trembling in the terrible troubles that beset him. Even Moses did not know how or for what he should pray—not knowing how the deliverance would be accomplished—but his cry came from his heart.

God intends that his promise and our prayer or yearning which is grounded in that promise should not be disdained or rejected, but be highly valued and esteemed. Further, God accomplishes much through the faith and longing of another, even a stranger, even though there is still no personal faith. But this is given through the channel of another's intercession, as in the gospel Christ raised the widow's son at Nain because of the prayer of his mother apart from the faith of the son. And he freed the little daughter of the Canaanite woman from the demon through the faith of the mother apart from the daughter's faith.

"Comfort for Women Who Have Had a Miscarriage" (1542)
LW 43, 248, 250

Friday

Be constant in prayer.
Romans 12:12 (Luther's translation)

This is spoken in opposition to those who only read the Psalms without any heart. And we must be on our guard that the prayers in church in our day do not become more of a hindrance than a help. First, because we offend God more by reading them when our heart is not in it, as He says: "This people honors Me with their lips, . . ." (Matt. 15:8; Mark 7:6; Isa. 29:13). Second, because we are deceived and made secure by the appearance of these things, as if we had truly prayed properly. And thus we never become really attached to the desire for true prayer, but when we pray these things, we think that we have prayed and are in need of nothing more. This is a terrible danger.

This is the reason why he inserted the word "constant," a great watchword that must be noted and respected by all, and especially by clerics. For this word signifies that we must put real work into our praying. And it is not in vain. For as the ancient fathers have said. "There is no work like praying to God."

Therefore, when believers want to enter the priesthood, they must first consider that they are entering a work which is harder than any other, namely, the work of prayer. For this requires a subdued and broken mind and an elevated and victorious spirit.

Lectures on Romans (1515–16)
LW 25, 458

WORSHIP

Lord God, I thank you for your great and beautiful goodness and grace which you have given us in the preaching of your word. You have instructed us to make use of it, especially on the sabbath day, for the meditation of the human heart can never exhaust such a treasure. Your word is the only light in the darkness of this life, a word of life, consolation, and supreme blessedness. Where this precious and saving word is absent, nothing remains but a fearsome and terrifying darkness, error and faction, death and every calamity, and the tyranny of the devil himself, as we can see with our own eyes every day. Amen.

LW 43, 202 (paraphrase)

Monday

These things I remember as I pour out my soul: how I went with the throng, and led them in procession to the house of God, with glad shouts and songs of thanksgiving, a multitude keeping festival.
Psalm 42:4

Now this multitude must have some kind of a room and its days or hours, which will be convenient for the listeners. Therefore God very wisely arranged and appointed things, and instituted the holy sacrament to be administered in the congregation at a place where we can come together, pray, and give thanks to God. Just as is done in worldly affairs when something which concerns the community must be dealt with, so much the more should this be done where we are to hear the Word of God.

And here the advantage is that when Christians thus come together their prayers are twice as strong as otherwise. One can and one really should pray in every place and every hour; but prayer is nowhere so mighty and strong as when the whole multitude prays together. Thus the dear patriarchs [and matriarchs] gathered with their families, and anybody else who happened to be with them, under a tree, or put up a tent, and erected an altar, and this was their temple and house of God, where they talked about Christ, the coming seed who was promised to them, sacrificed together, called upon God, and gave thanks to him. And thus they were always glad to be with the multitude whenever they could, even though they also meditated upon God's Word and promise and prayed by themselves in private.

"Sermon at the Dedication of the Castle Church in Torgau" (1544)
LW 51, 337–38

Observe the sabbath day and keep it holy,   **Tuesday**
as the LORD *your God commanded you.*
Deuteronomy 5:12

What does it mean to "keep holy" a day? Obviously it does not mean to sit in idleness and do nothing. It means rather, in the first place, to do something on that day which is a holy work, which is owing only to God, namely, that above all other things one preaches God's Word purely and holily, not as these scribes and Pharisees who falsify and pervert God's commandment. And likewise, that the others hear and learn God's Word and help to see to it that it is purely preached and kept. This is what it means rightly to observe the day of rest and to "consecrate" the place or the church.

Secondly, it means that we receive the Word of God, which we have heard in our hearts and with which we have thus been sprinkled, in order that it may bring forth power and fruit in us, and that we may publicly confess it and intend to hold onto it through life and through death.

Thirdly, it means that when we have heard God's Word we also lift up to God our common, united incense, that is, that we call upon him and pray to him together (which we know is certainly pleasing and acceptable to him, particularly in common assembly), and also praise and thank God together with joy for all his benefits, temporal and eternal, and all the wonderful works he does in his church. Thus everything that is done in such an assembly of the whole congregation or church is nothing but holy, godly business and work and is a holy sabbath, in order both that God may be rightly and holily served and all people be helped.

"Sermon at the Dedication of the Castle Church in Torgau" (1544)
LW 51, 342–43

Worship

Wednesday

At that time people began to invoke the name of the LORD. *Genesis 4:26b*

By worship of God Moses does not mean the ceremonies devised and handed down by men, not the statues which have been set up or other playthings of human reason, but calling upon the name of "the Lord." Here, then, we have the highest form of worship, which is pleasing to God and later on was commanded in the First Table of The Ten Commandments, and which included the fear of God, trust in God, confession, prayer, and preaching.

The First Commandment demands faith, that you believe that God is a Helper in due time, as Ps. 9:9 declares. The Second demands confession and prayer, that we call upon the name of God in danger and give thanks to God. The Third, that we teach the truth and defend and preserve sound doctrine. These are the true and only forms of worship of God which God demands; He does not demand sacrifices, money, and other things. He demands the First Table, that you hear, meditate on, and teach the Word; that you pray, and that you fear God. Whenever this is done, there will follow spontaneously, as it were, the forms of worship or the works of the Second Table. It is impossible for one who worships in accordance with the First Table not to keep the Second Table also.

Lectures on Genesis (1535–36)
LW 1, 328–29

Thursday

*For six days you shall continue to eat
unleavened bread, and on the seventh day
there shall be a solemn assembly for the
LORD your God, when you shall do no
work.   Deuteronomy 16:8*

Human nature tends unceasingly to set up ceremonies and institute
forms for worshiping God. Therefore it is necessary that it be curbed
and kept in the Word of God, through which we are sure that what
we do is divinely instituted and pleases God. The Old Testament
festivals also assure that the people come together at least two or three
times a year, hear and learn the Law of God, and be kept in the unity
of faith and life.

There are, however, three things which he wanted remembered
at these three festivals. In the Festival of Passover they should recall
the Exodus from Egypt. At the Pentecost Festival they should
remember receiving the Law on Mt. Sinai. At the Feast of Tabernacles
they were to remember all the physical benefits shown in those forty
years in the desert. So you see that the festivals are established for the
sake of our salvation and the glory of God, that the Word of God
may be heard and His blessings remembered, that we may be
instructed, nourished, and preserved in faith and love.

All these festivals we celebrate by an allegory of the Spirit in one
festival. For we observe the Passover every day when we proclaim
and believe that Christ, the Lamb of God was offered up for us. So
daily we have Pentecost when we receive the new Law, the Spirit,
into our hearts (Jer. 31:33) through the ministry of the Word. Daily
we celebrate the Feast of Tabernacles when we teach and experience
that we are strangers in this world and sojourn in the tabernacles of
our bodies which last but a short time.

Lectures on Deuteronomy (1523–25)
LW 9, 156–57

Friday

But the Lord answered her, "Martha, Martha, you are worried and distracted by many things; there is need of only one thing. Mary has chosen the better part, which will not be taken away from her."
Luke 10:41-42

Other matters concerning worship will adjust themselves as the need arises. This is the sum of the matter: Let everything in the worship service be done so that the Word may have free course instead of the prattling and rattling that has been the rule up to now. We can spare everything except the Word. Again, we profit by nothing as much as by the Word. For the whole Scripture shows that the Word should have free course among Christians. In Luke 10:42, Christ himself says, "One thing is needful," meaning that Mary sit at the feet of Christ and hear his word daily. This is the best part to choose and it shall not be taken away forever. It is an eternal Word. Everything else must pass away, no matter how much care and trouble it may give Martha. God help us achieve this. Amen.

"Concerning the Order of Public Worship" (1523)
LW 53, 14

OUR MISSION TO OTHERS

O Almighty God, dear heavenly Father, help that our good deeds and conduct may incite others to praise and honor you but not ourselves, exalting and praising your name because of us. Help us so that our evil actions and shortcomings may not offend anyone, leading them to dishonor your name or to neglect your praise.... Help us conduct all our life in such a way that we may be found to be true children of God, lest we call you Father falsely or in vain. Amen.

LW 43, 31

Monday

"This is my commandment, that you love one another as I have loved you. . . . You are my friends if you do what I command you." John 15:12, 14

It is surely kind and pleasing that Christ calls them His friends. For He would like to encourage and rouse us to pay heed to His love, to consider how He made the Father our Friend and how He proved Himself our Friend above all friends. But all of us who are His friends must also live in friendship with one another.

Thus He gives this kind commandment. The Lord, who gave body and soul and did everything for us, does not demand of us payment for this as though we had to do so for His sake. He asks that we do something in our own interest. From Him we have everything for nothing, and all that is required of us is that we help one another.

Christ says: "I ask you to love one another, to be loyally attached to one another, and to serve one another in a friendly way—all this in your own best interest. I am commanding you to do nothing more than to love one another as I have loved you. After all, it is only natural for you to do this, and it should be done spontaneously."

For it is natural—and everybody must admit this—that everyone would like to be shown love, fidelity, and help. Therefore we have been intermingled by God in order that we may live side by side and serve and help one another. God has no need whatever of such service and help, nor does He give this command for His sake. But we, of course, need it in our inmost hearts.

Sermons on the Gospel of St. John (1537)
LW 24, 251–53

For the whole law is summed up in a single commandment, "You shall love your neighbor as yourself." Galatians 5:14

Love is the highest virtue. It is neither called forth by anything that someone deserves nor deterred by what is undeserving and ungrateful. And no creature toward which you should practice love is nobler than your neighbor—that is, any human being especially one who needs your help.

This person is not a devil, not a lion or a bear, not a stone or a log. This is a living creature very much like you. There is nothing living on earth that is more lovable or more necessary. The neighbor is naturally suited for a civilized and social existence. Thus nothing could be regarded as worthier of love in the whole universe than our neighbor.

But such is the amazing craft of the devil that he is able not only to remove this noble object of love from my mind but even to persuade my heart of the exactly opposite opinion. My heart regards the neighbor as worthy, not of love but of the bitterest hatred. The devil accomplishes this very easily, suggesting to me: "Look, this person suffers from such and such a fault. The neighbor has chided you, has done you damage." Immediately this most lovable of objects becomes vile. My neighbor no longer seems to be someone who should be loved but an enemy deserving of bitter hatred.

In this way we are transformed from lovers into haters. All that is left to us of this commandment are the naked and meaningless letters and syllables: "You shall love your neighbor as yourself."

Lectures on Galatians (1535)
LW 27, 58

Wednesday

"In everything do to others what you would have them do to you; for this is the law and the prophets."   Matthew 7:12

With these words Christ concludes the teaching He has been giving in the Sermon on the Mount. He wraps it all up in a little package where it can all be found. Thus everyone can put it in his bosom and keep it.

It is as if He were saying: "Would you like to know what I have been preaching, and what Moses and all the Prophets teach you? I shall tell it to you so briefly and put it in such a way that you dare not complain about its being too long or too hard to remember." This is the kind of sermon that can be expanded or contracted. From it all teaching and preaching go forth and are broadcast, and here they come back together. How could it be put more succinctly and clearly than in these words?

The trouble is that the world and our old Adam refuse to let us ponder what He says and measure our lives against the standard of this teaching. We let it go in one ear and out the other. If we always measured our lives and actions against this standard, we would not be so coarse and heedless in what we do, but we would always have enough to do. We could become our own teachers, teaching ourselves what we ought to do.

Commentary on "The Sermon on the Mount" (1532)
LW 21, 235

For you say, "I am rich, I have prospered, and I need nothing." You do not realize that you are wretched, pitiable, poor, blind, and naked.   Revelation 3:17

Thursday

It is the worst kind of vice and the most demonic kind of pride for us to commend ourselves and pat ourselves on the back if we see or feel some special gift in ourselves. We do not thank God for it, but we become so proud and contemptuous of others and so preoccupied with it that we do not pay attention to whatever else we are doing, and imagine that we are in fine shape. We rob God of His glory this way, and we make ourselves an idol, without seeing the trouble we cause by all this. Look at what the Apocalypse says to a bishop who let himself think that he was more learned and better than others (Rev. 3:17).

If it is true that your gift is greater than somebody else's, this is as it must be, because your office is different, higher, and greater. But when you go on to use your gift as a mirror in which to admire yourself, you spoil it completely and make this sublime ornament filthier than everybody else's faults. The richer your gifts, the more abominable the perversion if you make them an idol. Thus you replace God with yourself in your own heart. You become arrogant toward your neighbor and so completely blind in everything that you can no longer know or see God or your neighbor or even yourself.

God did not give you your gifts for you to tickle yourself with them, but for you to help your neighbor with them when he needs it, and thus by your strength to bear his weakness, by your piety and honor to cover up his sin and to conceal his shame, as God through Christ has done for you and still does every day.

Commentary on "The Sermon on the Mount" (1532)
LW 21, 216–18

Friday

Thieves must give up stealing; rather let them labor and work honestly with their own hands, so as to have something to share with the needy.   Ephesians 4:28

Humans do not live for themselves alone in these mortal bodies to work for their bodies alone, but they live also for all of humanity on earth; rather, they live only for others and not for themselves. They cannot ever in this life be idle and without works toward their neighbors.

People, however, need none of these things for their righteousness and salvation. Therefore they should be guided in all their works by this thought and contemplate this one thing alone, that they may serve and benefit others in all that they do, considering nothing except the need and the advantage of their neighbors. Accordingly the Apostle commands us to work with our hands so that we may give to the needy, although he might have said that we should work to support ourselves.

This is what makes caring for the body a Christian work, that through its health and comfort we may be able to work, to acquire, and lay by funds with which to aid those who are in need, that in this way the strong member may serve the weaker, and we may be children of God, each caring for and working for the other, bearing one another's burdens and so fulfilling the law of Christ (Gal. 6:2). This is a truly Christian life. Here faith is truly active through love.

"The Freedom of a Christian" (1520)
LW 31, 364–65

VOCATION

*D*ear Lord, I have your Word, and I am in the station that pleases you. This much I know. You see all my inadequacies, and I know no help except in you. Help, therefore, because you have commanded that we should ask, seek, and knock, and have said that then we shall surely receive, find, and have what we want. Amen.

LW 21, 233

Vocation

Monday

Remember your leaders, those who spoke the word of God to you; consider the outcome of their way of life, and imitate their faith.   Hebrews 13:7

In God's sight this principle stands firm and unshakable: all saints live by the same Spirit and by the same faith, and are guided and governed by the same Spirit and the same faith, but they all do different external works. For God does not work through them at the same time, in the same place, in the same work, or in the sight of the same people. He moves at different times, in different places, in different works, and in different people, but he always rules them by the same Spirit and in the same faith.

And each one is compelled by the work, place, time, persons, and circumstances, previously unknown to him, to follow God as he rules and guides him. This is the true knowledge of faith in which all saints are instructed, each one in his own vocation.

Treatise on "The Judgment of Martin Luther on Monastic Vows" (1521)
LW 44, 269

Tuesday

There was also a prophet, Anna ... She was of a great age, having lived with her husband seven years after her marriage, then as a widow to the age of eighty-four. She never left the temple but worshiped there with fasting and prayer night and day.   Luke 2:36-37

It is a rather dangerous thing, if one looks only at the works and not at the person or station or calling. It is most unpleasing to God for someone to give up the duties of one's calling or station and to want to take up the works of the saints. Hence if a married woman should want to follow Anna and would forsake husband and children, house and parents, in order to go on a pilgrimage, to pray, to fast, and to go to church, she would only tempt God. To leave one's own calling and to attach oneself to alien undertakings, surely amounts to walking on one's ears and to turning everything upside down. Good works must be performed, and one should pray and fast to the extent that the work of one's calling and station are not neglected or impeded. Serving God is not tied to one or two works, nor is it confined to one or two callings, but it is distributed over all works and all callings.

Luke also writes that Anna lived seven years with her husband. By this expression he praises her married state and the duties of this estate also, so that nobody should get the idea that he considers only praying and fasting good works. For she did not do this while she was living with her husband, but only after she had become a lonely old widow.

You, likewise, must pay attention to your estate; you will find enough good works to do, if you wish to be pious. Every estate has enough works without needing to look for strange ones.

Sermon on "The Gospel for the Sunday after Christmas,
Luke 2[:33-40]" (1522)
LW 52, 124–25

Vocation

Wednesday

[Hagar] gave this name to the LORD who spoke to her: "You are the God who sees me," for she said, "I have now seen the One who sees me."
Genesis 16:13 (NIV)

The Word of God is never without fruit. Therefore the rebellious, proud, and disobedient Hagar is changed when the angel speaks. She returns to her mistress and patiently submits to her authority. Not only this; she acknowledges God's mercy, praises God, and calls upon Him by a new name in order to proclaim abroad the kindness through which He had manifested Himself to her.

This example is profitable for giving us instruction in order that all may come to know the kindnesses of God in their vocations, may be thankful for them and proclaim them. Likewise, that we may bear with patience the chastisements inflicted by our superiors, because God takes pleasure in such patience and sends help.

It is a sacrifice of thanksgiving and a service most pleasing to God if you acknowledge and proclaim His acts of kindness and call Him *He who sees me* as if you were saying: "I thought I had been completely forsaken by God. But now I see that He had regard for me and did not cast me aside when I was in trouble."

This is a most beautiful name for God. Would that we all could bestow it on Him. We would conclude with certainty that He has regard for us and cares for us, especially when He seems to have forgotten us. For he who can say in affliction: "God sees me" has true faith and can do and bear everything, yes, he overcomes all things and is triumphant.

Lectures on Genesis (1538)
LW 3, 69–70

"Blessed are those who mourn, for they will be comforted." Matthew 5:4

Thursday

Mourning and sorrow are not a rare plant among Christians, in spite of outward appearances. Daily, whenever they look at the world, they must see and feel in their heart so much wickedness, arrogance, contempt, and blasphemy of God and His Word, so much sorrow and sadness, which the devil causes in both the spiritual and the secular realm. Therefore they cannot have many joyful thoughts, and their spiritual joy is very weak. If they were to look at this continually and did not turn their eyes away from time to time, they could not be happy for a moment.

Simply begin to be a Christian, and you will soon find out what it means to mourn and be sorrowful. If you can do nothing else, then get married, settle down, and make a living in faith. Love the Word of God, and do what is required of you in your station. Then you will experience, both from your neighbors and in your own household, that things will not go as you might wish. You will be hindered and hemmed in on every side, so that you will suffer enough and see enough to make your heart sad. But especially the dear preachers must learn this well and be disciplined daily with all sorts of envy, hatred, scorn, ridicule, ingratitude, contempt, and blasphemy. In addition, they have to stew inside, so that their heart and soul is pierced through and continually tormented.

Those who mourn this way are entitled to have fun and to take it wherever they can so that they do not completely collapse for sorrow. Christ also adds these words and promises this consolation so that they do not despair in their sorrow nor let the joy of their heart be taken away and extinguished altogether, but mix this mourning with comfort and refreshment.

Commentary on "The Sermon on the Mount" (1532)
LW 21, 20–21

Friday

"Ask for whatever you wish, and it will be done for you."   John 15:7b

Open your mouth confidently, as a little child speaks to its father, who is pleased with everything it does if only it comes to him. The father is especially glad to comply with all the child's requests if it chats with him in a childlike manner when it asks him for something. Not only that, but he also provides for the child, and his one concern is to supply all the child's needs.

Hence Christians enjoy a great and glorious advantage if they remain pure and firm in the faith and guard against false doctrine and impure living. This is a splendid and comforting sermon on the estate of being a Christian.

Where is there a calling or walk of life on earth about which there are so many splendid promises as about this one? And these promises pertain to all who are called Christians and are baptized, whether monk or layperson, master or servant, mistress or maid, young or old. This must indeed be an estate blessed and prized above all others, to which the divine promise is assured that whatever those in it ask of and desire from God shall surely be granted and shall be yea and amen before God. Besides, everything that is done in this estate shall be approved and praised by God. Should we not be willing to wander to the ends of the earth in search of such a promise? Now it is carried before our very door without any toil or cost on our part, for the benefit of all who will accept it.

Sermons on the Gospel of St. John (1537)
LW 24, 239–40

FORGIVENESS

O my dear Lord Jesus Christ, you know my poor soul and my great failings, which I confess and deplore before you alone with an open heart. Alas, I find that I do not have the kind of will and resolution I certainly ought to have and that I am daily falling as a failing, sinful human being. And you know that I desire to have such will and resolution, but my enemy leads me bound and captive. Redeem me, a poor sinner, according to your divine will, from every evil and temptation. Strengthen and increase in me the true Christian faith; grant me grace to love my neighbor with all my heart, honestly and as I do myself, as my brother or sister. Grant me patience in persecution and in every adversity. You said to Saint Peter that he should forgive not only seven times and you have bidden us ask of you with confidence. So I come in reliance on this command and your promise, and confess and deplore before you all my trouble, for you are my true Pastor and the Bishop of my soul. Your will be done and be blessed forever. Amen.

What Luther Says, 3:1104–5, #3526

Monday

The next day [John] saw Jesus coming toward him and declared, "Here is the Lamb of God who takes away the sin of the world!"   John 1:29

Anyone who wishes to be saved must know that all his sins have been placed on the back of this Lamb! Therefore John points this Lamb out to his disciples, saying: "Do you want to know where the sins of the world are placed for forgiveness? Then don't resort to the Law of Moses or betake yourselves to the devil. There, to be sure, you will find sins, but sins to terrify you and damn you. But if you really want to find a place where the sins of the world are exterminated and deleted, then cast your gaze upon the cross. The Lord places all our sins on the back of this Lamb. . . ."

Therefore a Christian must cling simply to this verse and let no one rob him of it. *For there is no other comfort either in heaven or on earth to fortify us against all attacks and temptations, especially in the agony of death.*

Christ does bear the sin—not only mine and yours or that of any other individual, or only of one kingdom or country, but the sin of the entire world. And you, too, are a part of the world.

Sermon on the Gospel of St. John (1537–40)
LW 22, 163–64

For what the flesh desires is opposed to the Spirit, and what the Spirit desires is opposed to the flesh; for these are opposed to each other, to prevent you from doing what you want.   Galatians 5:17

Tuesday

I remember that Staupitz [Luther's friend and one-time superior] used to say: "More than a thousand times I have vowed to God that I would improve, but I have never performed what I have vowed. Hereafter I shall not make such vows, because I know perfectly well that I shall not live up to them. Unless God is gracious and merciful to me for the sake of Christ and grants me a blessed final hour, I shall not be able to stand before Him with all my vows and good works." This despair is not only truthful but is godly and holy. Whoever wants to be saved must make this confession with the mouth and with the heart.

The saints do not rely on their own righteousness. They gaze at Christ, their Propitiator. If there is any remnant of sin in the flesh, they know that this is not imputed to them but is pardoned. Meanwhile they battle by the Spirit against the flesh. This does not mean that they do not feel its desires at all; it means that they do not gratify them. Even though they feel the flesh raging and rebelling in them, they do not become downcast. No, they fortify themselves with their faith.

Therefore let none despair when they feel their flesh begin another battle against the Spirit, or if they do not succeed immediately in forcing their flesh to be subject to the Spirit. But let them be aroused and incited to seek forgiveness of sins through Christ and to embrace the righteousness of faith.

Lectures on Galatians (1535)
LW 27, 72–74

Wednesday
Guard the doors of your mouth from her who lies in your embrace.   Micah 7:5b

Here the prophet does not want suspicion and hatred to exist between spouses. He wants the utmost love and good will which cannot exist without mutual trust. And yet he wants a limit to this trust, because it can happen that it is mistaken. For your spouse is a human being. Although this spouse fears God and pays heed to His Word, nevertheless, because Satan, the enemy, is lying in wait everywhere and because human nature is weak, your spouse can fall and disappoint your hope somewhere.

When you foresee this with your mind, you will be readier to forgive, and you will be less distressed if anything happens contrary to what you had hoped. Thus love will remain, and harmony will not be disturbed. For nothing has happened that was not anticipated, and love is readiest to forgive. This is indeed a rare gift, but because you are a Christian, remember that this ought to be your attitude.

And so with others, Christians hate no one, and yet they trust no one. If others show them some kindness, they consider this an advantage and delight in it, nevertheless in such a way that if the kindness should cease or some adversity should occur, they would not be provoked or begin to hate the other person. For those who are taught by the Holy Scriptures realize what is in humanity, and for this reason they place complete trust in God and not in humans; yet they love all equally and show kindness to all, even to their enemies.

This, then, is solid friendship and the most steadfast love. It has its source, not in our judgment but in the Holy Spirit, who urges our minds to follow the Word.

Lectures on Genesis (ca. 1536)
LW 2, 299–302

If we confess our sins, he who is faithful **Thursday**
and just and will forgive us our sins and
cleanse us from all unrighteousness.
1 John 1:9

In this Christian Church, wherever it exists, is to be found the forgiveness of sins, that is, a kingdom of grace and of true pardon. For in it are found the gospel, baptism, and the sacrament of the altar, in which the forgiveness of sins is offered, obtained, and received. But this forgiveness of sins is not to be expected only at one time, as in baptism, but frequently, as often as one needs it, till death.

For this reason I have a high regard for private confession, for here God's word and absolution are spoken privately and individually to each believer for the forgiveness of sins, and as often as believers desire it they may have recourse to it for this forgiveness, and also for comfort, counsel, and guidance. Thus it is a precious, useful thing for souls, as long as no one is driven to it with laws and commandments. But sinners are to be left free to make use of it, according to their own needs, when and where they wish; just as we are free to obtain counsel and comfort, guidance and instruction when and where our need or our inclination moves us. Private confession is worthwhile as long as one is not forced to enumerate all sins but only those which oppress one most greviously, or those which a person will mention.

"Confession Concerning Christ's Supper" (1528)
LW 37, 368

Friday

You were running well; who prevented you from obeying the truth? Such persuasion does not come from the one who calls you.
Galatians 5:7-8

This comfort applies to all who, in their affliction and temptation, develop a false idea of Christ. For Satan has a thousand tricks and turns the comfort of Christ upside down by setting against it the example of Christ. He says: "But your life does not correspond to Christ's either in word or in deed. You have done nothing good." When this happens, one who has been assailed should be comforted this way: "Scripture presents Christ in two ways. First as a gift. If I take hold of Him this way, I shall lack nothing whatever. As great as He is, He has been made by God my wisdom, righteousness, sanctification, and redemption (1 Cor. 1:30). Even if I have committed many great sins, nevertheless, if I believe in Him, they are swallowed up by His righteousness.

"Secondly, Scripture presents Him as an example for us to imitate. But I will not let this Christ be presented to me as exemplar except at a time of rejoicing, when I am out of reach of temptations, so that I may have a mirror in which to contemplate how much I am still lacking, lest I become smug. But in a time of tribulation I will only see and hear Christ as a gift, as Him who died for my sins, who has bestowed His righteousness on me, and who accomplished and fulfilled what is lacking in my life."

Lectures on Galatians (1535)
LW 27, 33–34

CHRISTIAN DISCIPLINE

May Christ comfort all of you by his Spirit and strengthen and instruct you. Amen.

Letters, 147

Monday

Out of my distress I called on the LORD; the LORD answered me and set me in a broad place.   Psalm 118:5

Let all people know most assuredly and not doubt that God does not send them this distress to destroy them. He wants to drive them to pray, to implore, to fight, to exercise their faith. In this way they learn another aspect of God's person and accustom themselves to do battle even with the devil and with sin, and by the grace of God to be victorious. Without this experience we could never learn the meaning of faith, the Word, Spirit, grace, sin, death, or the devil. Were there only peace and no trials, we would never learn to know God Himself. In short, we could never be or remain true Christians. Trouble and distress constrain us and keep us within Christendom.

We read: "I called upon the Lord." You must learn to call. Do not sit by yourself or lie on a couch, hanging and shaking your head. Do not destroy yourself with your own thought by worrying. Do not strive and struggle to free yourself. Mourn and pray as this verse teaches. Likewise Psalm 141:2 says: "Let my prayer be counted as incense before Thee, and the lifting up of my hands as an evening sacrifice!" Here you learn that praying, reciting your troubles, and lifting up your hands arc sacrifices most pleasing to God. It is His desire and will that you lay your troubles before Him. He does not want you to multiply your troubles by burdening and torturing yourself. He wants you to be too weak to bear and overcome such troubles; He wants you to grow strong in Him. By His strength He is glorified in you. Out of such experiences people become real Christians.

"Commentary on Psalm 118" (1530)
LW 14, 60–61

O give thanks to the LORD, for he is good;
his steadfast love endures forever!
Psalm 118:1

Tuesday

You must not read the words "good" and "His steadfast love" with dull indifference. Nor dare you skim over them as some read the Psalter. No, you must bear in mind that these are vibrant, significant, and meaningful words. They express and emphasize one theme: God is good, but not as a human being is good. From the very bottom of His heart He is inclined to help and do good continually. He is not given to anger or inclined to punish except where necessary and where persistent, impenitent, and stubborn wickedness compels and drives Him to it. A human being would not delay punishment and restrain anger as God does; he would punish a hundred thousand times sooner and harder than God does.

This verse also serves to comfort us in all our misfortunes. We are such softies, such sapless sufferers. A pain in the leg can cause us to fill heaven and earth with our howls and wails, our grumbling and cursing. But the good God permits such small evils to befall us merely in order to arouse us snorers from our deep sleep and to make us recognize, on the other hand, the incomparable and innumerable benefits we still have.

We also are to look at our misfortunes in no other way than that with them God gives us a light by which we may see and understand His goodness and kindness in countless other ways. Then we conclude that such small misfortunes are barely a drop of water on a big fire or a little spark in the ocean.

Commentary on "Psalm 118" (1530)
LW 14, 47, 48–50

Wednesday

Come, my people, enter your chambers, and shut your doors behind you; hide yourselves for a little while.   Isaiah 26:20

God admonished the people here as in Psalm 4:4, when He said: "Be angry, but sin not; commune with your own hearts on your beds and be silent." Do not complain and cry out in times of persecution, but enter your chambers, keep quiet, do not be angry and impetuous. But pray to the Lord in secret and make your complaint to Him, as Peter says of Christ: "When He was reviled, He did not revile in return" (1 Pet. 2:23), but kept silent, that is, He entered into His chamber.

"Hide yourselves for a little while," that is: "Wait a little and endure, because My wrath and your persecution are sudden and last only a moment. Therefore, see to it that you bear it for a little while. Do not erupt, because none of our troubles in the world are everlasting but only transitory." These are the riches of divine consolation that support us in every kind of trouble.

Soon after these words He says: "For behold, the Lord is coming" (Isa. 26:21). The Lord will punish His persecutors and will not permit much blood of His saints to be shed.

Lectures on Isaiah (ca. 1528)
LW 16, 209–10

"I am the true vine, and my Father is the vinegrower. He removes every branch in me that bears no fruit. Every branch that bears fruit he prunes to make it bear more fruit." John 15:1-2

Thursday

This is a very comforting picture and an excellent, delightful personification. Here Christ does not present a useless, unfruitful tree to our view. No, He presents the precious vine, which bears much fruit and produces the sweetest and most delicious juice, even though it does not delight the eye. He interprets all the suffering which both He and His Christians are to experience as nothing else than the diligent work and care of a vinedresser.

This requires the art of believing and being sure that whatever hurts and distresses us does not happen to hurt or harm us but for our good and profit. We must compare this to the work of the vinedresser who hoes and cultivates his vine. If the vine could talk and saw the vinedresser chopping about its roots with a mattock and cutting wood from its branches with a pruning hook, it would say: "What are you doing? Now I must wither and decay. You are removing the soil from my roots and belaboring my branches with those iron teeth."

But God is not a tyrant. He is a pious Vinedresser who tends and works His vineyard with all faithfulness and diligence, and surely does not intend to ruin it. He does not let His vineyard stand there to be torn to pieces by dogs and wild sows; He tends it and watches over it. He is concerned that it bear well and produce good wine. Therefore He must hoe and prune so as not to chop and cut too deeply into the stem and the roots, take off too many branches, or trim off all the foliage. Let us be unafraid. Let us not be terrified by the prongs and teeth of the devil and the world; for God will not let them go beyond what serves our best interests.

Sermons on the Gospel of St. John (1537)
LW 24, 193–94, 199

Friday

For a brief moment I abandoned you.
Isaiah 54:7a

Who can believe this, that every one of our tribulations is momentary and that God's wrath is a point in time? Nobody can believe this; in our feeling every tribulation seems eternal although in the sight of God it is momentary. Our feelings, our heart and flesh, do not see the end, and therefore they do not believe that it is for a moment. When the wrath of God presses down on us, that point does not seem to be mathematical but eternal.

The highest remedy is to leave the appearance behind and to turn from the obvious to what is not obvious. Therefore He says here: "If only you would cling to Me and keep away from the obvious, which is only a point!" Then He continues: "With everlasting love I will have compassion on you." This is a most excellent comparison. The moment of tribulation and wrath is a small one, but the mercy is everlasting and perpetual.

Yes, learn how to make this globe. The forsakenness is the center, but the mercy is the endless orb. It is not a physical globe, but it pertains to faith and is perceived by the Word. Thus let us take care to be certain in the Word. Then in all outward afflictions we will know that they are a point and that the mercy of God is the endless circumference of the globe.

Lectures on Isaiah (1527–30)
LW 17, 238–39

GOOD WORKS

Almighty God, who are the protector of all who trust in you, without whose grace no one is able to do anything, or to stand before you: Grant us richly your mercy, that by your holy inspiration we may think what is right and by your power perform the same; for the sake of Jesus Christ our Lord. Amen.

LW 53, 136–37

Monday

"I give you a new commandment, that you love one another. Just as I have loved you, you also should love one another. By this everyone will know that you are my disciples, if you have love for one another."
John 13:34-35

To believers no law is given by which they become righteous before God, as St. Paul says in 1 Timothy 1:9, because they are alive and righteous and saved by faith. Believers need nothing further except to prove their faith by works. Truly, if faith is there, they cannot hold back; they prove themselves, break out into good works, confess and teach this gospel before the people, and stake their lives on it. Everything that they live and do is directed to their neighbor's profit, in order to help the neighbor—not only to attainment of this grace, but also in body, property, and honor. Seeing that Christ has done this for them, they thus follow Christ's example.

That is what Christ meant when at the last he gave no other commandment than love, by which people were to know who were his disciples and true believers. For where works and love do not break forth, there faith is not right, the gospel does not yet take hold, and Christ is not rightly known.

"Prefaces to the New Testament" (1522, revised 1546)
LW 35, 361

"Let your light shine before others, so that they may see your good works and give glory to your Father in heaven."
Matthew 5:16

Tuesday

What He calls "good works" here is the exercise, expression, and confession of the teaching about Christ and faith, and the suffering for its sake. He is talking about works by which we "shine." This shining is the real job of believing or teaching, by which we also help others to believe. These are the works whose necessary consequence must be "that the heavenly Father is honored and praised."

Matthew is not writing about ordinary works that people should do for one another out of love which he talks about in Matthew 25:35 ff. Rather he is thinking principally about the distinctly Christian work of teaching correctly, of stressing faith, and of showing how to strengthen and preserve it. This is how we testify that we really are Christians. The other works are not such a reliable criterion, since even sham Christians can put on the adornment of big, beautiful works of love.

Thus the most reliable index to a true Christian is this: if from the way he praises and preaches Christ the people learn that they are nothing and Christ is everything. It is the kind of work that cannot remain hidden. It has to shine and let itself be seen publicly. That is always why it alone is persecuted, for the world can tolerate other works. This also entitles it to be called a work through which our Father is recognized and praised.

These are the works that should be first and foremost. They should be followed by those pertaining to our relations with our neighbor in what are called "works of love," which shine, too, but only insofar as they are ignited and sustained by faith.

Commentary on "The Sermon on the Mount" (1532)
LW 21, 65–66

Wednesday

How can we escape if we neglect so great a salvation?   Hebrews 2:3a

In the Law there are very many works—they are all external—but in the Gospel there is only one work—it is internal—which is faith. Therefore the works of the Law bring about external righteousness; the works of faith bring about righteousness that is hidden in God.

Consequently, when the Jews asked in John 6:28: "What must we do, to be doing the works of God?" Christ draws them away from a large number of works and reduces the works to one. He says: "This is the work of God, that you believe in Him whom He has sent" (John 6:29). Therefore, the whole substance of the new law and its righteousness is that one and only faith in Christ.

Yet it is not so one-and-only and so sterile as human opinions are, for Christ lives. Not only lives but works, and not only works but reigns. Therefore it is impossible for faith in Him to be idle. It is alive, and it itself works and triumphs, and in this way works flow forth spontaneously from faith.

For in this way our patience flows from the patience of Christ, and our humility from His, and the other good works in like manner, provided that we believe firmly that He has done all these things for us, not only for us but also before our eyes, that is as St. Augustine is wont to say, not only as a sacrament but also as an example.

"Lectures on Hebrews" (1517–18)
LW 29, 123

Good Works

Rescue the weak and the needy; deliver them from the hand of the wicked.
Psalm 82:4

Thursday

Who is the person at whose door and into whose house such good works do not present themselves every day? There is no need for him to travel far or inquire about good works.

But you might ask, "Why does God not do it all by himself, since he is able to help everyone and knows how to help everyone?" Yes, he can do it; but he does not want to do it alone. He wants us to work with him. He does us the honor of wanting to effect his work with us and through us. And if we are not willing to accept such honor, he will, after all, do the work alone, and help the poor. And those who were not willing to help him and who despised the great honor of doing his work he will condemn along with the unrighteous as those who made common cause with the unrighteous. Although he alone is blessed, he does us the honor of wanting to share his blessedness with us.

"Treatise on Good Works" (1520)
LW 44, 51–52

Friday

You shall not steal.   Exodus 20:15

This commandment also has a work which includes very many good works while opposing many vices. In German this work is called "selflessness," a willingness to help and serve all people with one's own means.

It was not in vain that the wise man said, "Happy is the rich man who is found without blemish, who has not run after gold, and has not set his confidence in the treasures of money. Who is he? We will praise him because he has performed a miracle in his life" (Ecclus. 31:8-9). Yes, there certainly are very few who notice and recognize such lust for gold in themselves. For greed can have a very pretty and attractive cover for its shame; it is called provision for the body and the needs of nature. Under this cover greed insatiably amasses unlimited wealth.

But if the heart expects and puts its trust in divine favor, how can a person be greedy and anxious? Such people are absolutely certain that they are acceptable to God: therefore, they do not cling to money; they use their money cheerfully and freely for the benefit of their neighbor.

In fact, in this commandment it can clearly be seen that all good works must be done in faith and proceed from faith. People are generous because they trust God and never doubt but that they will always have enough. In contrast, people are covetous and anxious because they do not trust God. Now faith is the master workman and the motivating force behind the good works of generosity, just as it is in all the other commandments.

"Treatise on Good Works" (1520)
LW 44, 106–9

STRENGTH IN WEAKNESS

Behold, Lord, here is an empty cask that needs to be filled. My Lord, fill it. I am weak in faith; strengthen me. I am cold in love; warm me and fill me with fire that my love may flow out over my neighbor. I do not have a firm, strong faith; I doubt at times and cannot fully trust God. O Lord, help me; increase my faith and trust for me. In you is locked the treasure of all my possessions. I am poor; you are rich and have come to have mercy upon the poor. I am a sinner; you are righteous. I pour forth a stream of sin; but in you are all fullness and righteousness. Amen.

What Luther Says, 3:1105, #3527

Strength in Weakness

Monday

The LORD says to my lord, "Sit at my right hand until I make your enemies your footstool."   Psalm 110:1

Observe this for your comfort: here these enemies are never called our enemies, or those of Christendom, but enemies of the Lord Christ. "Your enemies," he says, although they really attack Christendom and Christians must suffer and be plagued by them, as it actually happens. For Christ, who sits above at the right hand of the Father, cannot be attacked. They cannot hurt one hair on His head, much less drag Him down from His throne. Still they are properly called His enemies, not ours.

For the world and the devil do not attack and plague us because of secular matters or because we have merited or caused it. The only reason for it is that we believe this Lord and confess His word. For this reason He must deal with them as enemies who attack His person. Everything that happens to the individual Christian, whether it comes from the devil or from the world, such as the terrors of sin, anxiety and grief of the heart, torture, or death, He regards as though it happened to Him. He also says through the prophet Zechariah (Zech. 2:8): "He who touches you touches the apple of My eye." And in Matthew 25:40 we read: "As you did it to one of the least of these My brethren, you did it to Me."

Though we may feel the terrors of sin, anxiety and grief of heart, torture, and death, we are to remember that these are not our enemies but the enemies of our Lord, who is of our flesh and blood. We are to view Him as the Enemy of our enemies. In this comfort we are to direct them away from ourselves to Christ: "Do you not know? God has already judged you and pronounced you the footstool of Christ."

Commentary on "Psalm 110" (1535)
LW 13, 262

In returning and rest you shall be saved; in quietness and in trust shall be your strength.   Isaiah 30:15b

Tuesday

Translate it thus: "If you will sit down and be quiet, you shall be saved. Do not lose heart and do not lose your temper. Wait till the storm blows over and keep still." Now that is a marvelous victory, to conquer by sitting and waiting! Meanwhile the flesh runs and toils and looks for help.

But trust in God, be patient, and commit everything to Him. In a wonderful way you will see God as your protector. This passage is, therefore, an outstanding, golden, and magnificent promise: "In sitting quietly you shall be saved." Be calm, wait, wait, commit your cause to God, He will make it succeed. Look for Him a little at a time; wait, wait. But since this waiting seems long to the flesh and appears like death, the flesh always wavers. But keep faith. Patience will overcome wickedness.

The prophet further impresses this when he says: "Blessed are all those who wait for Him" (Isa. 30:18). That is to say, they who wait for God are the holy, the good, and the godly. These wait for God, even when He takes His time. Therefore the blessed are saved. Everything would turn out all right, if you could only wait. Therefore, in all trouble let us wait for God and we shall be blessed.

Lectures on Isaiah (ca. 1528)
LW 16, 258–61

Wednesday

Have you not known? Have you not heard? The LORD is the everlasting God, the Creator of the ends of the earth. He does not faint or grow weary.
Isaiah 40:28

This is a wonderful proclamation concerning God—He does not faint or grow weary. This seems mad to reason. But the prophet is depicting God in terms of our senses, as if he were saying: "We get tired and are worn out by Satan's plotting and cunning tricks. But you have a God who does not get tired. He will set you free from the incessant stratagems of Satan." Satan and the world are our relentless enemies. They keep after us until at last they exhaust us.

Therefore God consoles those who labor and are wearied: "I will not become weary. I have always been active, I am fresh and new. I can help you." Remembering this a certain nun by the name of Mechtild kept repelling the onslaughts of Satan with one word: "I am a Christian."

So I, too, must say: "I am dead, but Christ lives; I am a sinner, but Christ is righteous. I believe in Jesus Christ and was baptized in His name." Thus when we are fatigued, let us run to the fresh and untiring Christ and not remain with ourselves.

Lectures on Isaiah (1527–30)
LW 17, 30

Strengthen the weak hands.
Isaiah 35:3a

Thursday

This is a wonderful comfort that is to be understood not in a physical but in an internal sense, because it shines under the appearance of the cross. The members of the church are exposed to all, to Satan and to the craftiness and power of the world and the flesh. Therefore the prophet comforts them with exceedingly great consolations.

Strengthen the weak hands, he commands. Give medicine to those hands that are so weary, so that you become strong again. For Satan has two ways of fighting. He would gladly cast the faithful down suddenly from their joy and faith and into fear and despair. Secondly, he cunningly strives by long lasting torments and by the unremitting pressure of the torments to tire them out. These attacks are extremely powerful, and against Satan's continuous attack we must set our continuous divine help. The devil is a spirit at leisure and thinks of nothing but to take us by storm. We ought not have slack and idle hands over against his deceptions.

We ought to strengthen ourselves with these words and say, "Though all devils were rolled into one, my God is still greater." The afflicted must be comforted with such spiritual consolations of the Word, not with fleshly comfort which does nothing for troubled consciences. With spiritual comfort and with the living Word of God, the afflicted are made strong.

Lectures on Isaiah (ca. 1528)
LW 16, 300–1

Friday

He gives power to the faint.
Isaiah 40:29a

Here you must understand what it means to be faint and impotent, in opposition to carnal reason which wants to be strong and most powerful. Reason willingly hears one thing—that God gives strength, but it does not want to be worn out and nothing. So all the self-righteous willingly receive strength from God, but they do not want to be faint, as if God would not give strength to the weary. What need is there for the secure to receive strength?

But God gives strength to the weary, the oppressed, and the troubled. The emphasis lies on the word "faint," but we look for the stress on the word "power." It is as if God were saying: "You must be weary and emptied, so that there is no way out for you. Then I will give you strength. First you must become nothing, then consolation and strength will come."

Therefore let us learn to console ourselves when we are afflicted and say, "What I do not have and what I cannot do, that Christ has and can do."

Lectures on Isaiah (1527–30)
LW 17, 31

GRACE

O Father, we are faint and ill, and the trials in the flesh and in the world are severe and manifold. O dear Father, hold us and do not let us fall into temptation and sin again, but give us grace to remain steadfast and fight valiantly to the end. Without your grace and your help, we are not able to do anything. Amen.

LW 42, 80

Monday

There is therefore now no condemnation for those who are in Christ Jesus.
Romans 8:1

Between grace and gift there is this difference. Grace actually means God's favor, or the good will which in himself he bears toward us, by which he is disposed to give us Christ and to pour into us the Holy Spirit with his gifts. The gifts and the Spirit increase in us every day, but they are not yet perfect since there remain in us the evil desires and sins that war against the Spirit. Nevertheless grace does so much that we are accounted completely righteous before God. For his grace is not divided or parceled out, as are the gifts, but takes us completely into favor for the sake of Christ our Intercessor and Mediator. And because of this, the gifts are begun in us.

"Preface to the Epistle of St. Paul to the Romans" (1522, revised 1546)
LW 35, 369–70

For your name's sake, O LORD, preserve **Tuesday**
my life. In your righteousness bring me out
of trouble . . . for I am your servant.
Psalm 143:11-12

I live in grace. Therefore my whole life serves Thee, not myself, for I seek not myself but Thee and Thine. Those who live in their own righteousness cannot do this. They serve themselves and look for their own welfare in all things.

Now someone might say to me: "Can't you ever do anything but speak only about the righteousness, wisdom, strength of God rather than of humanity, always expounding Scripture from the standpoint of God's righteousness and grace, always harping on the same string and singing the same old song?"

I answer: Let each one look to himself. As for me, I confess: Whenever I found less in the Scriptures than Christ, I was never satisfied; but whenever I found more than Christ, I never became poorer. Therefore it seems to me to be true that God the Holy Spirit does not know and does not want to know anything besides Jesus Christ, as He says of Him (John 16:13-14): "He will glorify Me; He will not speak of Himself, but He will take of Mine and declare it to you."

Christ is God's grace, mercy, righteousness, truth, wisdom, power, comfort, and salvation, given to us by God without any merit on our part. Christ, I say, not as some express it in blind words, "causally," that He grants righteousness and remains absent Himself, for that would be dead. Yes, it is not given at all unless Christ Himself is present, just as the radiance of the sun and the heat of fire are not present if there is no sun and no fire.

Commentary on "The Seven Penitential Psalms" (1525)
LW 14, 204

Grace

Wednesday

He will not cry or lift up his voice, or make it heard in the street.   Isaiah 42:2

The prophet says that Christ Himself will not be noisy in the streets nor make Himself heard in the open. How does this jibe? The noise is of two kinds: the noise of wrath and that of love. He did indeed cry in the preaching proceeding from love, but not in a noisy way, as the self-righteous and other sects are noisy. In opposition to their harshest clamor the prophet depicts the office of Christ as being most gentle and mild. This is to cry without being noisy, that is, teach gently without rage.

In other partisan groups and judgments and lawsuits there is nothing but accusation and shouting on the part of those who suffer wrong on both sides. Even judges shout when they pass sentence. Thus the self-righteous are most turbulent. Because all of them are by nature sad and stern, all of them are ready to pass judgment. They measure everything by the standard of their own life and most severely condemn everything else.

True righteousness, however, has compassion, while the false has condemnation. Here in Christ you see the gentlest and most agreeable appearance. This is what it means for Christians not to raise their voices, that is, in an uproar, but rather in grace.

Lectures on Isaiah (1527–30)
LW 17, 64

And why not say (as some people slander us by saying that we say), "Let us do evil so that good may come"? Romans 3:8

Thursday

The apostle is not speaking primarily against those who are open sinners. He is speaking against those who appear righteous in their own eyes and trust in their own works for salvation. He is trying to encourage these people to magnify the grace of God, which cannot be magnified unless sin which is forgiven through this grace is first acknowledged and magnified.

This is why the others, when they heard this, were offended and thought that the apostle is preaching that evil should be done, so that the glory of God might be magnified. For in this way do our iniquity and our lying "Abound to His glory" (v. 7), when we, humbled through the confession of them, glorify God, who has forgiven such wickedness out of His overflowing grace. He would not be glorified in this way if we did not believe that we are in need of His grace but thought that we were sufficient of ourselves in His sight. Thus those are better off who acknowledge that they have many sins and no righteousness than those who like a Pharisee acknowledge that they have much righteousness and no sin. For the one glorifies the mercy of God, but the other their own righteousness.

Lectures on Romans (1515–16)
LW 25, 28

Grace

Friday
[The Son of God] loved me and gave himself for me.   Galatians 2:20b

Read these words "me" and "for me" with great emphasis. Accustom yourself to accepting this "me" with a sure faith and applying it to yourself. Do not doubt that you belong to the number of those who speak this "me."

It is as though Paul were saying: "The Law did not love me. It did not give itself for me. It accuses and frightens me. Now I have Another, who has freed me from the terrors of the Law, from sin, and from death. He is One who has transferred me into freedom, the righteousness of God, and eternal life. He is called the Son of God."

Therefore Christ is not Moses, not a taskmaster or a lawgiver. He is the Dispenser of grace, the Savior, and the Pitier. In other words, He is nothing but sheer, infinite mercy, which gives and is given.

For Christ is the joy and sweetness to a trembling and troubled heart. He is the One "who loved *me* and gave Himself for me."

Christ did not love only Peter and Paul, but the same grace belongs and comes to us. We are included in this *"me."* For just as we cannot deny that we are sinners, so we cannot deny that Christ died for our sins.

Lectures on Galatians (1535)
LW 26, 177–79

CHRIST IN US

O heavenly Father, give us our daily bread (our Lord Jesus Christ who feeds and comforts the soul) so that Christ may remain in us eternally and we in him, and that we may worthily bear the name of Christian as derived from Christ. Amen.

LW 43, 34, 35

Monday

[I pray] that Christ may dwell in your
hearts through faith.   Ephesians 3:17a

How then do we have Christ? Ah, you cannot have him except in the gospel in which he is promised to you. And since Christ comes into our heart through the gospel, he must also be accepted by the heart. As I now believe that he is in the gospel, so I receive him and have him already. So Paul says: I carry Christ in my heart, for he is mine. (cf. Eph. 3:17).

When we have Christ by true faith, then he causes us to live in such a way that we are strengthened in faith, in such a way that I do these works which I do for the benefit and good of my neighbor. For my Christian name would not be sufficient, despite my baptism and my faith, if I did not help my neighbors and draw them to faith through my works in order that they may follow me. Then believers, after they have given all glory to Christ, are always remembering to do to their neighbor as Christ has done to them, in order that they may help the neighbor and everyone else. Thus Christ lives in them and they live for the betterment of their neighbor, giving to everyone a good example of doing all things in love.

"Two Sermons Preached at Weimar" (The Second) (1522)
LW 51, 114, 116

I have been crucified with Christ; and it is no longer I who live, but it is Christ who lives in me.   *Galatians 2:19b-20a*

Tuesday

Who is this "I" of whom Paul says: "Yet not I"? It is the one that has the Law and is obliged to do works, the one that is a person separate from Christ. This "I" Paul rejects; for "I" as a person distinct from Christ, belongs to death and hell. That is why he says: "Not I, but Christ lives in me." Christ is my "form," which adorns my faith as color or light adorns a wall. "Christ," he says, "is fixed and cemented to me and abides in me. The life that I now live, He lives in me. Indeed, Christ Himself is the life that I now live. In this way, therefore, Christ and I are one."

Living in me as He does, Christ abolishes the Law, damns sin, and kills death; for at His presence all these cannot help disappearing. Christ is eternal Peace, Comfort, Righteousness, and Life, to which the terror of the Law, sadness of mind, sin, hell, and death have to yield. Abiding and living in me, Christ removes and absorbs all the evils that torment and afflict me. This attachment to Him causes me to be liberated from the terror of the Law and of sin, pulled out of my own skin, and transferred into Christ and into His kingdom, which is a kingdom of grace, righteousness, peace, joy, life, salvation, and eternal glory. Since I am in Him, no evil can harm me.

Lectures on Galatians (1535)
LW 26, 167

Wednesday

*Light rises in the darkness for the upright;
the Lord is gracious, merciful, and
righteous.*
Psalm 112:4 (Luther's translation)

Light, joy and pleasure, all things, are received by upright believers from Him who is gracious, merciful, and righteous toward them. It is based on their conviction that their hearts are right with Him who is good, gracious, and merciful. Then they have no misgivings but are confident.

The hypocrites and the wicked also call God gracious, merciful, and righteous. But they do not understand it. They read and sing and preach about it, but there is a big difference. It is one thing to preach, sing, and say that God is all these things. It is quite another to feel the gracious, merciful, and righteous God in the heart. The pious and upright have this not only on their tongue but also in their heart. When the tongue and the heart agree, then it is well. But if this lies in the mouth alone, and the heart is a hundred thousand miles away, then it is futile. Christians feel and experience it in their heart that those matters do not happen accidentally or come from mortals. They feel it in their heart, are sure about it, and do not doubt.

Now, they who feel this in their heart will be satisfied. The light rises for them in the darkness. When the darkness is past, they also become rich and rise high, even if they are poor and oppressed. For they have Him who is gracious and merciful. Now, if they have Him who is the Fountain and Source of all things, what could they lack?

Commentary on "Psalm 112" (1526)
LW 13, 391, 405

"If you abide in me, and my words abide   **Thursday**
in you . . ."   John 15:7a

Note how highly this Man extols the Christian life. In case someone has not understood and would like to ask: "But how, my dear Man, does one remain in Christ? How am I a branch in this Vine, or how do I remain a branch?"

Christ answers: "Just pay attention to My Word. Everything depends on whether My Word remains in you, that is whether you believe and confess the article taught in the children's (Apostles') Creed: 'I believe in Jesus Christ, our Lord, who was crucified for me, who died, rose again, and is seated at the right hand of the Father,' and whatever pertains to it. If you remain faithful to this and are ready to stake all on it, to forsake all rather than accept a different doctrine or works, if you thus remain in the Word, then I remain in you and you in Me. Then our roots are intertwined; then we are joined, so that My words and your heart have become one. Then you will not ask further how I abide in you or you in Me, for you will see this in yonder life. Now, however, you can grasp and comprehend it in no other way than that you have My Word, that you are washed in My blood by faith, and that you are anointed and sealed with My Spirit. Therefore your whole life and all your deeds are acceptable and nothing but good fruit."

Sermons on the Gospel of St. John (1537)
LW 24, 238–39

Friday

First, I thank my God through Jesus Christ for all of you, because your faith is proclaimed throughout the world.
Romans 1:8

This is the Christian and true way of praising people—not to praise people for their own sake but to praise God in them first and foremost and to attribute everything to Him, as Isaiah 43:21 says: "This people have I formed for Myself, they shall show forth My praise."

Then the apostle shows that God is not praised except through Christ. As we receive everything from God through Him so we must return everything to God through Him since He alone is worthy to appear before the face of God and to carry on His priestly office for us, as in Hebrews 13:15: "Through Him then let us continually offer up a sacrifice of praise to God, that is, the fruits of lips that acknowledge His name."

Therefore, he praises God through Christ for these people. While it is characteristic of envy to be sad about a neighbor's good gifts and to curse them, here we see love. For it is the nature of love that it rejoices in the good gifts of the neighbor, especially his spiritual gifts, and glorifies God in them.

Lectures on Romans (1515–16)
LW 25, 6–7

FALL

THE LORD'S PRAYER

[God] you do not wish us just to call you Father but that we all, together, should call on you, Our Father. Therefore grant us a harmonious loving kindness so that we may all regard and accept each other as true brothers and sisters and turn to you as the dear Father of us all, praying for all persons as one child might entreat its father for someone else. And let none of us seek only our own advantage in prayer before you, forgetting the other person, but let us strip ourselves of all hatred, envy, and discord, and love each other as true and reverent children of God, and thus all repeat together not my *Father, but* our *Father. Amen.*

LW 43, 30

Monday

"When you are praying, do not heap up empty phrases.... Pray then in this way: Our Father in heaven ..."
Matthew 6:7, 9a

Prayer requires first that one lay before God the needs or perils, all of which are included in the Lord's Prayer. The first three petitions deal with the most important matters of all. We do not pray the petitions like clods, who pay no heed to the magnitude of the things we pray for, who seek only food for the belly, gold, and so forth, not caring about how we may become good, how we may have the pure Word and live holy lives, not caring that the will of God is hindered by the devil, who throws himself athwart to prevent its being done.

We pray, therefore, that he trample the devil under foot and subject us to himself. Likewise there is great need to pray for the bread we eat, for grain, cattle, and the like, and for all that we have, in order that we may know that all this comes to us from God. But we are always falling down and hence we have a bad conscience; therefore we pray: "Forgive us our trespasses." In these seven petitions are found all our anxieties, needs, and perils, which we ought to bring to God. They are great petitions, indeed, but God, who wills to do great things, is greater. Therefore, let us learn to pray well since God wants us to do this. Then we shall experience the power of God, through which he is able to give us great things, to make us good, to keep the Word, to give us a holy life and all else. He allows such manifold perils to come upon us in order that we may learn to pray and experience his help in our great evils. This is our great consolation.

"Ten Sermons on The Catechism" (1528)
LW 51, 181

"Our Father in heaven, hallowed be your name. Your kingdom come. Your will be done, on earth as it is in heaven."
Matthew 6:9b-10

Tuesday

What we pray is: Dear Father, defend us from the devil and his cohorts and from our lazy flesh which would hinder your will, and grant grace that your gospel may go forth unhindered. Thus we are shown in these three petitions our need with regard to God, but in such a way that it redounds to our benefit. God's name is not only hallowed in itself, but in me. Likewise, God's kingdom not only comes of itself and his will is done not only of itself, but rather in order that God's kingdom may come in me, that God's will may be done in me, and his name be hallowed in me.

"Ten Sermons on The Catechism" (1528)
LW 51, 175

The Lord's Prayer

Wednesday

"For if you forgive others their trespasses, your heavenly Father will also forgive you; but if you do not forgive others, neither will your Father forgive your trespasses."
Matthew 6:14-15

This is a remarkable addition, but a very precious one. Someone may wonder why He should append this addition to "Forgive us our debts." He could just as well have appended some such item to one of the other petitions. He could have said: "Give us our daily bread, as we give it to our children."

By putting the petition this way, connecting the forgiveness of sin with our forgiving, He makes mutual love a Christian obligation. The continual forgiveness of the neighbor is the primary and foremost duty of Christians, second only to faith and the reception of forgiveness.

Christ attached this addition to the prayer to establish the closest possible bonds between us and to preserve His Christendom in the unity of the Spirit (Eph. 4:3), both in faith and in love. We must not let any sin or fault divide us or rob us of our faith and of everything else. It is inevitable that there be friction among us every day in all our social and business contacts. Things are said that you do not like to hear and things are done that you cannot stand. This gives rise to anger and discord. We still have our flesh and blood about us, behaving in its own way and easily letting slip an evil word or an angry gesture or action, which is an affront to love.

Therefore there must be continual forgiveness among Christians, and we continually need forgiveness from God, always clinging to the prayer: "Forgive us, as we forgive."

Commentary on "The Sermon on the Mount" (1532)
LW 21, 148–49, 154–55

"And lead us not into temptation."
Matthew 6:13a (NIV)

Thursday

The first temptation is that of the flesh, which says: Go ahead and have illicit intercourse with another's wife, daughter, maid! That is Master Flesh. Or he says: I'm going to sell the grain, beer, or goods as dearly as I can. This is the temptation of the flesh. Here the greed of our flesh is seeking its own advantage. Then you should pray: Guard us, dear Lord, from temptation! Likewise, the flesh seeks to satisfy its lust in glutting, guzzling, and loafing.

Next is the world, which tempts you with envy, hatred, and pride. Your neighbor irritates you to anger when you are making a bargain and all of a sudden there is impatience, the nature of the world—up she goes, blow your top, and it's all off! Then one conforms to the world. These are worldly temptations. Therefore pray: O Lord, bring it to pass that the flesh and the world shall not seduce me! Both of them, the flesh and the world, contribute much toward your feeling an inclination to spite and lechery and dislike for your neighbor.

The third companion and tempter is Master Devil. He tempts you by causing you to disregard God's Word: Oh, I have to look after the beer and malt, I can't go to hear a sermon. Or if you do come to church to hear the sermon you go to sleep, you don't take it in, you have no delight, no love, no reverence for the Word. When you feel such temptations, go running to the Lord's Prayer! You have the promise that God will deliver you from the temptation of the flesh, the world, and the devil. Therefore pray: Father, let not our flesh seduce us, let not the world deceive us, let not the devil cast us down.

"Ten Sermons on The Catechism" (1528)
LW 51, 179–80

The Lord's Prayer

Friday

"But deliver us from evil."
Matthew 6:13b (RSV)

Now note that deliverance from evil is the very last thing that we do and ought to pray for. Under this heading we count strife, famine, war, pestilence, plagues, even hell, in short, everything that is painful to body and soul. Though we ask for release from all of this, it should be done in a proper manner and at the very last.

Why? There are some, perhaps many, who honor and implore God solely for the sake of deliverance from evil. They have no other interest and do not ever think of the first petitions which stress God's honor, his name, and his will. Instead, they seek their own will and completely reverse the order of this prayer. They begin at the end and never get to the first petitions. They are set on being rid of their evil, whether this redounds to God's honor or not, whether it conforms to his will or not.

An upright believer, however, says, "Dear Father, evil and pain oppress me. I suffer much distress and discomfort. I am afraid of hell. Deliver me from these, but only if this is to your honor and glory and if it agrees with your divine will. If not, then your will, and not mine, be done [Luke 22:42]. Your divine honor and will are dearer to me than my own ease and comfort, both now and eternally." Now that is a pleasing and good prayer and is certain to be heard in heaven.

"An Exposition of the Lord's Prayer for Simple Laymen" (1519)
LW 42, 75

BIBLE STUDY

Almighty and most merciful God . . . , grant that our study of [the Bible] may not be made in vain by the callousness or carelessness of our hearts, but that by it we may be confirmed in penitence, lifted in hope, made strong for service, and above all filled with the true knowledge of you and of your Son Jesus Christ. Amen.

Minister's Prayer Book, 156, #258
(George Adam Smith)

Monday

Praise the LORD, all you nations! Extol him, all you peoples! For great is his steadfast love toward us, and the faithfulness of the LORD endures forever. Praise the LORD!
Psalm 117

This is a short, easy psalm, doubtless made this way so that everyone might pay more attention to it and remember better what is said. No one can complain about the length or content, much less about the sharpness, difficulty, or profundity of the words. Here we find only short, precise, clear, and ordinary words, which everyone can understand if he will only pay attention and think about them.

All God's words demand this. We must not skim over them and imagine we have thoroughly understood them like the frivolous, smug, and bored souls do. When they hear some word of God once, they consider it old hat and cast about for something new. This is a dangerous disease, a clever and malicious trick of the devil. Thus he makes people bold, smug, forward, and ready for every kind of error and schism.

All this, as I see it, is the result of reading and listening to God's word carelessly instead of concentrating on it with fear, humility, and diligence.

I have often felt this particular devil and temptation myself. But I dare not say in my heart: "The Lord's Prayer is worn out; you know the Ten Commandments; you can recite the Creed." I study them daily and remain a pupil of the Catechism. I feel, too, that this helps me a lot, and I am convinced by experience that God's Word can never be entirely mastered, but that Ps. 147 speaks truly; "His understanding is beyond measure" (v. 5), or Ecclesiasticus: "Who drinks of me shall thirst even more after me" (24:29).

Commentary on "Psalm 117" (1530)
LW 14, 7–8

Keep these words that I am commanding
you today in your heart.
Deuteronomy 6:6

Tuesday

Not only in a book, not only in thought, he says, but in the inmost feeling should these words be the most precious treasure. For where your treasure is, there will your heart be also (Matt. 6:21). Therefore let nothing reign in your heart except faith and the love of God. On these let your heart meditate day and night (Ps. 1:2).

For where they have first been in the heart in this way, there it will follow happily that they are also in your mouth. "And impress them on your sons" [Deut. 6:7]; that is, repeat and ingrain these words of faith daily, lest they become pale and cold, and grow old with rust.

Then it will follow that you will speak of them everywhere and always. Finally, bind them as a memorial on your hands and before your eyes; last of all write them on the doorposts. [Deut. 6:8-9]

See the order of treating the Word of God: first, it is to be pondered in the heart; secondly, impressed faithfully and constantly on children by word of mouth; thirdly, discussed openly and everywhere; fourthly, written on the hand and drawn before the eyes—that is, fulfilling them in deed and pondering them; fifth and last, inscribed, and that on posts and doorways, not in books, since Moses himself has already written them in a book. He simply wants these words to meet us everywhere and to be in our memories.

Lectures on Deuteronomy (1523)
LW 9, 69

Wednesday

"Come, let us go up to the mountain of the LORD, . . . that he may teach us his ways." Isaiah 2:3

Here nothing but the sweetness of the Word is discussed; one can never learn enough. Paul says in Col. 3:16: "Let the Word of Christ dwell in you richly"; that is one must ponder it constantly, and always some new fire to arouse the heart will be found. Christians never read the same teaching enough. For the Gospel does not concern itself with knowledge; it concerns itself with feeling. But we slip every day. The flesh, sin, death, and the world assail us. Not for even one moment are we safe from spiritual adultery. This is how it is because sins surround us on all sides and weaken godly feelings. Besides, the world persecutes us.

Hence it is necessary to hear the Word of God constantly, in order that our feelings may be enlightened. At another place He says (Matt. 6:13): "And lead us not into temptation, but deliver us . . ." For no one is safe for even one hour, but all are daily in a most precarious state. Now they stand, now they fall, and now an evil conscience. Therefore, Christians must live every day by the Word as the body lives by food. That one who does not have the Word or ponder it soon becomes a sorry wretch. If I do not reflect on a verse of a psalm or a statement of the Gospel, my heart is completely full of sins. A return to the Word guards against sins. The heart is always grinding. If the grain, namely, the Word of God, is good, the flour will be good, and the bread will be good.

Lectures on Isaiah (ca. 1528)
LW 16, 30–31

Bible Study

Thursday

For I handed on to you as of first importance what I in turn had received: that Christ died for our sins in accordance with the scriptures, and that he was buried, and that he was raised on the third day in accordance with the scriptures.
1 Corinthians 15:3-4

Note how Paul again extols and exalts the testimony of Scripture and the external Word as he emphasizes and repeats the phrase "according to the Scriptures." He does this in the first place to resist the mad spirits who disdain Scripture and the external message and in place of this seek other secret revelation. And today every place is also teeming with such spirits, confused by the devil, who regard Scripture a dead letter and boast of nothing but the Spirit, although these people retain neither Word nor Spirit.

But here you notice how Paul adduces Scripture as his strongest proof, for there is no other enduring way of preserving our doctrine and our faith than the physical or written Word, poured into letters and preached orally by him or others. And the Holy Spirit must work through this in the heart, and the heart must be preserved in the faith through and in the Word against the devil and every trial. Otherwise, where this is surrendered, Christ and the Spirit will soon be lost. The Holy Spirit, as you know, has deposited His wisdom and counsel and all mysteries into the Word and revealed these in Scripture, so that no one can excuse himself. Nor must anyone seek or search for something else or learn or acquire something better or more sublime than what Scripture teaches of Jesus Christ, God's Son, our Savior, who died and rose for us.

Commentary on "1 Corinthians 15" (1534)
LW 28, 76–77

Friday

O give thanks to the LORD, for he is good;
his steadfast love endures forever.
Psalm 118:1

Lest any, knowing that this psalm belongs to the whole world, raise their eyebrows at my claim that this psalm is mine, may they be assured that no one is being robbed. After all, Christ is mine, and yet He belongs to all believers. I will not be jealous but will gladly share what is mine. Would to God all the world would claim this psalm for its own, as I do! Peace and love could not compare with such a friendly quarrel. Sad to say, there are few, even among those who should do better, who honestly say even once in their lifetime to Scripture or to one of the psalms: "You are my beloved book; you must be my very own psalm."

The neglect of Scripture, even by spiritual leaders, is one of the greatest evils in the world. Everything else, arts or literature, is pursued and practiced day and night, and there is no end of labor and effort. But Holy Scripture is neglected as though there were no need of it. Those who condescend to read it want to absorb everything at once. There has never been an art or a book on earth that everyone has so quickly mastered as the Holy Scriptures. But its words are not, as some think, mere literature; they are words of life, intended not for speculation and fantasy but for life and action. But why complain? No one pays any attention to our lament. May Christ our Lord help us by His Spirit to love and honor His holy Word with all our hearts. Amen. I commit myself to your prayer.

Commentary on "Psalm 118" (1530)
LW 14, 46

CHRISTIAN FREEDOM

I pray you, dear Father, grant us your grace that we and all others may treat each other in kindly, gentle, charitable ways, forgiving one another from the heart, bearing each other's faults and shortcomings in a Christian and loving manner, and thus living together in true peace and concord, as the commandment teaches and requires us to do. Amen.

LW 43, 205–6 (paraphrase)

Monday

For though I am free with respect to all, I have made myself a slave to all, so that I might win more of them.
1 Corinthians 9:19

To make the way smoother for the unlearned—for only them do I serve—I shall set down the following two propositions concerning the freedom and the bondage of the spirit:

A Christian is a perfectly free lord of all, subject to none.

A Christian is a perfectly dutiful servant of all, subject to all.

These two theses seem to contradict each other. If, however, they should be found to fit together they would serve our purpose beautifully. Both are Paul's own statements, who says in 1 Cor. 9:19, "For though I am free from all . . . I have made myself a slave to all," and in Rom. 13:8, "Owe no one anything, except to love one another." Love by its very nature is ready to serve and be subject to the one who is loved. So Christ, although he was Lord of all, was "born of woman, born under the law" (Gal. 4:4), and therefore was at the same time free and a servant, "in the form of God" and "of a servant" (Phil. 2:6-7).

So a Christian, like Christ his head, is filled and made rich by faith and should be content with this form of God which he has obtained by faith. This faith is his life, his righteousness, and his salvation: it saves him and makes him acceptable, and bestows upon him all things that are Christ's. Although Christians are thus free from all works, they ought in this liberty to empty themselves, take upon themselves the form of a servant, be made in human likeness, be found in human form, and to serve, help, and in every way deal with their neighbor as they see that God through Christ has dealt and still deals with them.

Treatise on "The Freedom of a Christian" (1520)
LW 31, 344, 366

Jesus answered them, "Very truly, I tell you, everyone who commits sin is a slave to sin." John 8:34

Tuesday

Christ does not plan to alter secular kingdoms or to abolish serfdom. What does He care how princes and lords rule? It does not concern Him how a person plows, sows, makes shoes, builds houses, or pays tribute or taxes. Such work was ordered in Gen. 1:28, when God created the world and specified that we should beget children and occupy and cultivate the world. Here Christ is not speaking about these external matters; rather He is speaking of a freedom which lies outside and above this outward existence and life. Here He deals with freedom from sin, death, God's wrath, the devil, hell, and eternal damnation.

This Christian freedom may be enjoyed both by one who is free and by one who is a bondservant, by one who is a captive and by one who takes others captive, by a woman as well as by a man, by a servant and a maid as well as by a lord and a lady. We are speaking of the freedom before God, the freedom we have when God pronounces us free from sin. This freedom is extended to all.

Sermons on the Gospel of St. John (1530–32)
LW 23, 404

Christian Freedom

Wednesday

For freedom Christ has set us free. Stand firm, therefore. Galatians 5:1a

Christ has set us free, not from some human slavery or tyrannical authority but from the eternal wrath of God. Where? In the conscience. This is where our freedom comes to a halt; it goes no further. For Christ has set us free, not for a political freedom or a freedom of the flesh but for a theological or spiritual freedom. Our conscience is free and joyful, unafraid of the wrath to come (Matt. 3:7). This is the most genuine freedom, it is immeasurable. For who can express what a great gift it is for someone to be able to declare for certain that God neither is nor ever will be wrathful but will forever be a gracious and merciful Father for the sake of Christ?

It is a great and incomprehensible freedom that is easier to talk about than it is to believe. If this freedom Christ has achieved for us could be grasped in its certainty, no fury or terror of the world, the Law, sin, death, the devil, could be too great. For it would swallow them up as quickly as the ocean swallows a spark. This freedom of Christ certainly swallows up and abolishes a whole heap of evils and in their place it establishes righteousness, peace, life and more. Blessed is the one who understands and believes this.

Lectures on Galatians (1535)
LW 27, 4–5

They are like trees planted by streams of water, which yield their fruit in its season.
Psalm 1:3a

To bring forth fruit indicates that these blessed ones, through love, serve not themselves but their neighbors. They are compared to a tree which bears fruit not for itself, but for others. In fact, no creatures live for themselves or serve only themselves except human beings and the devil. The sun does not shine for itself, water does not flow for itself. Certainly every creature serves the law of love, and its whole substance is in the Law of the Lord. Even the members of the human body do not serve only themselves. Only the passions of the heart are ungodly. For this ungodly passion not only gives none their own, serves no one, is kind to no one, but snatches everything for itself, looks for its own in everything, even in God Himself. But these blessed ones possess the kindness of the good trees, which do no one evil but help everyone, while willingly giving their fruits.

The blessed ones give these fruits "in their season." Oh, this is a golden lovable word, through which the freedom of the righteous Christian is affirmed! The ungodly have fixed days, fixed times, certain works, and certain places to which they are so firmly bound that even if their neighbor were to die of starvation, they could not tear themselves away to help. But the blessed ones are free at all times, in every work, for every place, and toward every person. Whatever the situation, they will serve you; and whatever their hands find to do, they will do it. They give their fruit in its season, as often as God or other people need their works.

"Psalm 1" (1519)
LW 14, 300–1

Christian Freedom

Friday

And the life I now live in the flesh I live by faith in the Son of God, who loved me and gave himself for me.
Galatians 2:20b

He ought to think: "Although I am unworthy and condemned, my God has given me in Christ all the riches of righteousness and salvation without any merit on my part, out of pure, free mercy, so that from now on I need nothing except faith which believes that this is true. Why should I not therefore freely, joyfully, with all my heart, and with an eager will do all things which I know are pleasing and acceptable to such a Father who has overwhelmed me with his inestimable riches? I will therefore give myself as a Christ to my neighbor, just as Christ offered himself to me. I will do nothing in this life except what I see is necessary, profitable, and salutary to my neighbor, since through faith I have an abundance of all good things in Christ."

Behold, from faith thus flow forth love and joy in the Lord, and from love a joyful, willing, and free mind that serves one's neighbor willingly and takes no account of gratitude or ingratitude, of praise or blame, of gain or loss. For believers do not serve that they may put others under obligations. They do not distinguish between friends and enemies or anticipate their thankfulness or unthankfulness, but they most freely and most willingly spend themselves and all that they have, whether they waste all on the thankless or whether they gain a reward.

Therefore, if we recognize the great and precious things which are given us, our hearts will be filled by the Holy Spirit and the love which makes us free, joyful, almighty workers and conquerors over all tribulations, servants of our neighbors, and yet lords of all.

Treatise on "The Freedom of a Christian" (1520)
LW 31, 367

THE HIDDEN GOD

*God, O God? Do you not hear me, my God? Are you dead?
No, you cannot die; you are merely hiding yourself. . . . O God,
stand by me in the name of your dear Son, Jesus Christ, who
shall be my Protector and Defender, yes, my mighty Fortress,
through the might and the strengthening of your Holy Spirit.*

What Luther Says, 3:1108, #3539

The Hidden God

Monday

In the beginning when God created the heavens and the earth, . . .   Genesis 1:1

Some have asked: What was God doing before the beginning of the world: Was He in a state of rest or not? Augustine relates in his *Confessions* that someone had answered to this effect: "God was making hell ready for those who pried into meddlesome questions," obviously, as Augustine says, to frustrate any injurious effect of the question.

Let us, therefore, rid ourselves of such ideas and realize that God was incomprehensible in His essential rest before the creation of the world, but that now, after the creation, He is within, without, and above all creatures; that is, He is still incomprehensible. Nothing else can be said, because our mind cannot grasp what lies outside time.

It is folly to argue much about God outside and before time, because this is an effort to understand the Godhead without a covering, or the uncovered divine essence. Because this is impossible, God envelops Himself in His works in certain forms, as today He wraps Himself up in Baptism, in absolution, and other such forms.

It is therefore insane to argue about God and the divine nature without the Word or any covering, as all the heretics are accustomed. Whoever desires to be saved and to be safe when dealing with such great matters, let that one simply hold to the form, the signs, and the coverings of the Godhead, such as His word and His works. For in His Word and in His works He shows Himself to us. Those who are in touch with these are made sound, as was the woman with the issue of blood when she touched Christ's garment (Matt. 9:20-22).

Lectures on Genesis (1535–36)
LW 1, 10–11, 13

A wind from God swept over the face of the waters.   Genesis 1:2b

Tuesday

Those who want to reach God apart from these coverings exert themselves to ascend to heaven without ladders (that is, without the Word). Overwhelmed by His majesty, which they seek to comprehend without a covering, they fall to their destruction.

Therefore if we want to walk in safety, let us accept what the Word submits for our reflection and what God Himself wants us to know. Let us pass by the other things—things not revealed in the Word. What concern is it of mine, and how can I comprehend what God did before the earth was created? These are thoughts concerning the uncovered Godhead.

When God reveals Himself to us, it is necessary for Him to do so through some such veil or wrapper such as creation or reconciliation and to say: "Look! Under this wrapper you will be sure to take hold of Me." When we embrace this wrapper, adoring, praying, and sacrificing to God there, we are said to be praying to God and sacrificing to Him properly.

Thus Isaiah says that [in his vision] he saw the Lord in a very wide garment (6:1). [That is, Isaiah saw the greatness of God's robe, not God himself], because God cannot be depicted or viewed in a vision which is absolute. Therefore such figures of speech have the approval of the Holy Spirit, and the works of God are set before us so that we can grasp them. Such works are: that He created the heaven and the earth, that He sent His Son, that He speaks through His Son, that He baptizes, that He absolves from sin through the Word. Whoever does not apprehend these facts will never apprehend God.

Lectures on Genesis (1535–36)
LW 1, 14–15

The Hidden God

Wednesday

[The LORD said to Moses,] "Then I will take away my hand, and you shall see my back; but my face shall not be seen."
Exodus 33:23

One must debate either about the hidden God or about the revealed God. With regard to God, insofar as He has not been revealed, there is no faith, no knowledge, and no understanding. And here one must hold to the statement that what is above us is none of our concern. For thoughts of this kind, which investigate something more sublime above or outside the revelation of God, are altogether devilish. With them nothing more is achieved than that we plunge ourselves into destruction; for they present an object that is inscrutable, namely, the unrevealed God. Why not rather let God keep His decisions and mysteries in secret? We have no reason to exert ourselves so much that these decisions and mysteries be revealed to us.

Moses, too, asked God to show him His face; but the Lord replies: "You shall see My back, but you will not be able to see My face." For this inquisitiveness is original sin itself, by which we are impelled to strive for a way to God through natural speculation. But this is a great sin and a useless and futile attempt; for Christ says: "No one comes to the Father but by Me." Therefore when we approach the unrevealed God, then there is no faith, no Word, and no knowledge; for He is an invisible God, and you will not make Him visible.

God wanted to counteract this curiosity for this is how He set forth His will and counsel: "Behold, this is My Son; listen to Him. Look at Him as He lies in the manger and on the lap of His mother, as he hangs on the cross. Observe what He does and what He says. There you will surely take hold of Me." For "He who sees Me," says Christ, "also sees the Father Himself."

Lectures on Genesis (1541–42)
LW 5, 44–45

The Hidden God

No one has ever seen God. It is God the only Son, who is close to the Father's heart, who has made him known.   John 1:18

Whence comes the knowledge of the God of grace and truth? It is given by the only-begotten Son of God. The Son of God, who is in God and who Himself is God, is indispensable for this. For He comes from the Father, and He knows the truth. There is no other doctor, teacher, or preacher who resides in the Godhead and is in the bosom of the Father but the one Doctor, Christ. He who is in the divine essence descends from heaven to us and becomes human.

Who else could have revealed God to us? Consult all the law books of the jurists, all the books of the philosophers and of all heathen. You will find that they do not exceed the knowledge of God contained in the Law of Moses, enjoining us not to steal, not to commit perjury, and to love government and parents. To know God from the Law with His back turned to us is a left-handed knowledge of Him.

Therefore walk around God and behold His true countenance and His real plan—God is seen properly only in Christ. There we learn that all who wish to be saved must confess that they are damnable sinners, and that they must rely on Him who is full of grace and truth. Thus they also attain grace and truth; this is the true mind of God. We must depend on Christ; this is the true knowledge of God. Through the only-begotten Son and through the Gospel one learns to look directly into God's face.

Sermons on the Gospel of St. John (1537–40)
LW 22, 156–57

The Hidden God

Friday

Grace to you and peace from God our Father and the Lord Jesus Christ. Galatians 1:3

But why does the apostle add "and the Lord Jesus Christ"? Did it not suffice to say "from God the Father"? Why does he link Jesus Christ with the Father? You have often heard from us that it is a rule and principle in the Scriptures, and one that must be scrupulously observed, to refrain from speculation about the majesty of God, which is too much for the human body, and especially for the human mind to bear.

But true Christian theology, as I often warn you, does not present God to us in His majesty, as Moses and other teachings do, but Christ born of the Virgin as our Mediator and High Priest. Therefore when we are embattled against the Law, sin, and death in the presence of God, nothing is more dangerous than to stray into heaven with our idle speculations, there to investigate God in His incomprehensible power, wisdom, and majesty, to ask how He created the world and how He governs it. If you attempt to comprehend God this way and want to make atonement to Him apart from Christ the Mediator, making your works and fasts the mediation between Him and yourself, you will inevitably fall, as Lucifer did (Isa. 14:12), and in horrible despair lose God and everything. Take hold of God as Scripture instructs you (1 Cor. 1:21, 24): "Since, in wisdom, the world did not know God through wisdom, it pleased God through the folly of what we preach to save those who believe. We preach Christ crucified, a stumbling block to Jews and folly to Gentiles, but to those who are called, both Jews and Greeks, Christ the power of God and the wisdom of God."

Lectures on Galatians (1535)
LW 26, 28–29

SAINT AND SINNER

To his love I, a sinner, commend you, a sinner, for you confess your sins and do not defend them. Amen.

Letters, 159

Monday

Greet every saint in Christ Jesus.
Philippians 4:21a

The Holy Scriptures call Christians saints and the people of God. It is a pity that it's forgotten that we are saints, for to forget this is to forget Christ and baptism.

You say that the sins which we commit every day offend God, and therefore we are not saints. To this I reply: Mother love is stronger than the filth and scabbiness on a child, and so the love of God toward us is stronger than the dirt that clings to us. Accordingly, although we are sinners, we do not lose our filial relation on account of our filthiness, nor do we fall from grace on account of our sin.

"Table Talk recorded by Veit Dietrich" (1533)
LW 54, 70

And Ham, the father of Canaan, saw the nakedness of his father, and told his two brothers outside.   *Genesis 9:22*

Tuesday

All this serves for our instruction. Because at times God permits even righteous and holy persons to stumble and fall either into actual offenses or into such as seem so, we must be on our guard lest we immediately pass judgment, as Ham did. He had despised his father long since, but only now does he do so openly. Moreover, he maintains that his father is feeble-minded from senility and has evidently been forsaken by the Holy Spirit, because he, on whom lay the rule of the church, state, and the home, has not refrained from drunkenness. But, O wretched Ham, how happy you are that now at last you have found what you were seeking, namely, poison in a lovely rose!

God should be praised and blessed forever for dealing with His saints in a truly wonderful manner. For while He permits them to be weak and to stumble, while He lets them abound with actions that result in displeasure and offense, and the world judges and condemns them, He forgives them these weaknesses and has compassion on them. On the other hand, He leaves to Satan and utterly rejects those who are angels in their own eyes.

Hence when we see saints fall, let us not be offended. Much less let us gloat over the weakness of other people, or rejoice, as though we were stronger, wiser, and holier. Rather let us bear with and cover, and even extenuate and excuse, such mistakes as much as we can, bearing in mind that what the other person has experienced today we may perhaps experience tomorrow. We are all one mass, and we are all born of one flesh.

Lectures on Genesis (ca. 1536)
LW 2, 169, 171

Wednesday

The disagreement became so sharp that they parted company. Acts 15:39a

Paul and Barnabas had been set aside for the ministry of the Gospel among the Gentiles and had traveled through many areas and announced the Gospel. Yet Luke testified that there came such a sharp disagreement between them that they parted company. Here there was a fault either in Paul or in Barnabas. It must have been a very sharp disagreement to separate such close companions, and this is what the text suggests. Such examples are written for our comfort. For it is a great comfort for us to hear that even such great saints sin—a comfort which those who say that saints cannot sin would take away from us.

Samson, David and many other celebrated leaders who were full of the Holy Spirit fell into huge sins. Such errors and sins of the saints are set forth in order that those who are troubled and desperate may find comfort and that those who are proud may be afraid. No one has ever fallen so grievously as to not have stood up again. On the other hand, no one has such a sure footing that he or she cannot fall. If Peter fell, I, too, may fall; if he stood up again, so can I.

Lectures on Galatians (1535)
LW 26, 108–9

*So I find it to be a law that when I want
to do what is good, evil lies close at hand.
Romans 7:21*

St. Cyprian, in a sermon on the sickness unto death, finds here his comfort when thinking of his sins and says, "Ceaselessly, we must fight against avarice, unchastity, anger, and ambition. Steadfastly and with toil and sorrow we must wrestle with carnal desires and the enticements of the world. The human mind, surrounded and besieged by the assaults of the devil, can scarcely meet or resist them all. If avarice is prostrated, unchastity springs up. If lust is overcome, ambition takes its place. If ambition is despised, then anger is provoked, pride puffs up, drunkenness takes the offensive, hatred breaks the bonds of unity, jealousy breaks up friendship. The human spirit must suffer many persecutions and the heart must expect many perils."

Let us understand this properly! Believers cannot pray against sin and about sin or have such a desire to be free from sin, unless they are already godly. Only the Spirit who in Baptism has just begun his work and incipient grace are so constituted that they work against the sin which remains. Believers would like to be altogether godly, but cannot achieve this because of the resistance of the flesh. But those who have never begun to be godly do not struggle or lament or pray against their flesh and sin. They feel no resistance, but go on and follow where the flesh leads.

"Defense and Explanation on All the Articles" (1521)
LW 32, 22–23

Friday

Those who eat my flesh and drink my blood abide in me, and I in them.
John 6:56

Christ wants to indicate that many people have heard Him, can converse about Him, and cling to Him so long as all goes well. But to remain with Him, to abide in Him and make their dwelling in Him, to confess Him with heart and lips when it really counts—that is no child's play or trifle. The true presence and greatness of faith are evinced when a person in the midst of life's storms neither speaks nor acts differently from the way the Christ who is in him speaks and acts. This is something that transcends human strength and human work.

Outwardly Christians stumble and fall from time to time. Only weakness and shame appear on the surface, revealing that the Christians are sinners who do that which displeases the world. Then they are regarded as fools, as Cinderellas, as footmats for the world, as damned, impotent, and worthless people. But this does not matter. In their weakness, sin, folly, and frailty there abides inwardly and secretly a force and power unrecognizable by the world and hidden from its view, but one which, for all that, carries off the victory; for Christ resides in them and manifests Himself to them. I have seen many of these who, externally, tottered along very feebly, but when it came to the test and they faced the court, Christ bestirred Himself in them, and they became so staunch that the devil had to flee.

Sermons on the Gospel of St. John (1530–32)
LW 23, 145–47

TEMPORAL GOODS

O Lord God, heavenly Father, I am your creature; do with me whatever you please; it is all the same to me, for I know that I am surely yours. And if it please you that I die this hour or suffer some great misfortune, I would still be very glad to suffer it. Never do I want to consider my life, honor, goods, and whatever I have as higher and greater than your will. Your will shall please me at all times throughout my life. Amen.

What Luther Says, 3:1105, #3529

Monday

"Give to everyone who begs from you, and do not refuse anyone who wants to borrow from you."   Matthew 5:42

The second degree of dealing with temporal goods is that we are to give freely and without return to anyone who needs our goods or asks for them. Of this our Lord Jesus Christ says in Matthew 5:42, "Give to everyone who begs from you." Although this degree is much lower than the first (giving away all our temporal goods), it is nevertheless hard and bitter to those who have more taste for temporal than eternal goods. They have not enough trust in God to believe that he can or will sustain them in this wretched life. They therefore fear that they would die of hunger or be ruined entirely if they were to obey God's command and give to everyone who asks of them. How then can they trust him to maintain them in eternity?

As Christ says, "One who does not trust God in a little matter, will never trust him in something greater." Nevertheless, they go ahead and suppose that God will save them eternally. They even think that in this regard they have perfect trust in him. Yet they will not heed this commandment of his by which he would train and drive them to learn to trust him in things temporal and eternal.

Hence, there is reason to fear that one who will not listen to this teaching and follow it will never acquire the art of trusting, and that those who will not trust God in little temporal things must at last despair also in those matters that are great and eternal.

Treatise on "Trade and Usury" (1524)
LW 45, 280–81

"Give to everyone who begs from you; . . . **Tuesday**
Do to others as you would have them do
to you." Luke 6:30-31

There are common practices among us that stand in the way of Christian giving. The first is that people give and present things to their friends, and to the rich and powerful who do not need them, but forget the needy.

Another practice has a beautiful, brilliant appearance, but it does the most harm to this giving. The lofty title of "alms" and of "giving for God's sake" is bestowed solely on giving for churches, monasteries, chapels, altars, towers, bells, organs, paintings, images, silver and gold ornaments and vestments, and the like. Giving has taken hold here, and the real stream of giving runs in the direction toward which people have guided it and where they wanted to have it. No wonder, then, that in the direction toward which Christ's word guides it things are so dry and desolate. Where there are a hundred altars or vigils there is not a single person who feeds a tableful of poor people or in other respects assists a needy household.

Now we would not disallow the building of suitable churches and their adornment; we cannot do without them. And public worship ought rightly to be conducted in the finest way. But there should be a limit to this, and we should take care that the appurtenances of worship be pure, rather than costly. It would be satisfactory if we gave the smaller proportion to churches, altars, vigils, bequests, and the like and let the main stream flow toward God's commandments, so that among Christians charitable deeds done to the poor would shine more brightly than all the churches of wood and stone.

Treatise on "Trade and Usury" (1524)
LW 45, 282–86

Wednesday

"Blessed are the poor in spirit."
Matthew 5:3a

The doctrine and life of the whole world are founded only upon their having enough. Such a doctrine can only make people greedy, so that everyone is interested in nothing but amassing plenty and in having a good time, without need or trouble. And everyone concludes: "If that person is blessed who succeeds and has plenty, I must see to it that I do not fall behind."

Therefore Christ preaches a totally new sermon here for the Christians. Something is necessary other than the possession of enough on earth. But you say: "What? Must all Christians, then, be poor? Dare none of them have money, property, popularity, power, and the like? What are the rich to do? Must they surrender all their property and honor, or buy the kingdom of heaven from the poor?"

No. It does not say that whoever wants to have the kingdom of heaven must buy it from the poor. The little word "spiritually" is added. Nothing is accomplished when someone is physically poor and has no money or goods. The command is to be "spiritually poor." He wants to discuss only the spiritual—how to live before God, above and beyond the external.

There is the example of David. He was an outstanding king, and he really had his wallet and treasury full of money, his barns full of grain. In spite of all this he had to be a poor beggar spiritually, as he sings of himself (Ps. 39:12), "I am poor, and a guest in the land." This is truly a heart that does not tie itself to property and riches.

Commentary on "The Sermon on the Mount" (1532)
LW 21, 11–13

"For where your treasure is, there your heart will be also."   *Matthew 6:21*

Thursday

Now Christ concludes with a proverb, saying: "Where your treasure is, there will your heart be also." This is equivalent to what we Germans say about a greedy belly: "Money is his heart"; that is, if only he has money, that is his joy and his comfort, in other words, his god. On the other hand, when he has nothing, that is death for him; then there is no heart, no joy, no comfort.

What He means is this: "Keep watch on your own heart, and test it. And be assured that your heart will be in the same place where your treasure is." As the common saying has it, "What is dear to you, that is your god." It is to this that your heart draws you; you think about it day and night; you go to sleep with it, and you wake up with it, whether it is money or property, pleasure or fame.

So take a look at your own heart, and you will soon find out what has stuck to it and where your treasure is. It is easy to determine whether hearing the Word of God, living according to it, and achieving such a life gives you as much enjoyment and calls forth as much diligence from you as does accumulating and saving money and property.

Commentary on "The Sermon on the Mount" (1532)
LW 21, 175–76

Temporal Goods

Friday

Now Abram was very rich in livestock, in silver, and in gold.   Genesis 13:2

The philosophers and the monks have often found fault with this passage and have wondered why the Holy Spirit records that Abraham was rich or greatly encumbered with the possession of cattle, silver, and gold. Both arrive at the opinion that so holy a man should not have had any wealth but should have lived in poverty, as befits someone who has put all his hope in the mercy of the one and only God, especially since he was an exile.

The philosophers indeed believed that they would achieve a great reputation if they disposed of their money and called themselves beggars. The monks did the same thing. Why is this? It is because they observe that through the use of wealth people generally become worse. Therefore they suppose that it would be advisable for them to condemn wealth and refrain from it altogether.

If it were a virtue to cast possessions away and to be a beggar, Abraham would be praised without deserving it. But now he keeps on managing and using his possessions, and his special effort is to keep his heart pure. He does not become proud because of his wealth and does not gain and preserve it in a greedy manner; but he is generous and hospitable.

As for you, reform your mind, and use these things with a sincere heart. If God has given you wealth, give thanks to God, and see that you make the right use of it.

Lectures on Genesis (ca. 1536)
LW 2, 325–26, 329, 331

CHILDREN

Dear Lord, I commend to you my household and family. Grant that I may care for them as a Christian should. Defend us against the Destroyer and all his wicked angels who would do us harm and mischief in this life. Amen.

LW 43, 196–97 (paraphrase)

Children

Monday

Noah did this; he did all that God commanded him.   Genesis 6:22

Noah is praised as an example for us because he did not have a dead faith, which is actually no faith at all, but a living and active faith. The particular praise of Noah's faith is that he stays on the royal road; he adds nothing, changes nothing, and takes nothing away from God's directive but abides completely by the command he hears.

God has the habit of commanding ordinary, unimportant, laughable, and at times even offensive things. Reason, however, takes delight in what is magnificent; either it is filled with disgust at those common things, or it undertakes them with resentment. Thus the tasks of a householder have filled some people with disgust, and they have assigned to themselves other tasks, which are more magnificent in appearance.

But the person who considers the One who gives the commands will surely regard as most important even those things that seem most trivial. To be a spouse, to rear children—these things some regard as something unimportant. And yet experience shows that they are most important attainments, which human wisdom cannot achieve at all. We see that at times even the most spiritual people have failed shamefully. If, then, we consider Him who gives the command, it will readily become clear that even though God's commands appear ordinary and trivial, they are nevertheless of the highest order and cannot be carried out or fulfilled by any human being except with divine help.

Lectures on Genesis (ca. 1536)
LW 2, 77–79

Those who love [their children] are diligent to discipline them.
Proverbs 13:24b

Tuesday

This at least all married people should know. They can do no better work and do nothing more valuable either for God, for Christendom, for all the world, for themselves, and for their children than to bring up their children well. In comparison with this one work, that married people should bring up their children properly, there is nothing at all in pilgrimages to Rome or Jerusalem, nothing at all in building churches, endowing masses, or whatever good works could be named. For bringing up their children properly is their appointed work. Where parents are nonconscientious about this, it is as if everything were the wrong way around, like fire that will not burn or water that is not wet.

You could do no more disastrous work than to spoil the children, let them curse and swear, let them learn profane words and vulgar songs, and just let them do as they please. What is more, some parents use enticements to be more alluring to meet the dictates of the world of fashion, so that they may please only the world, get ahead, and become rich, all the time giving more attention to the care of the body than to the due care of the soul. There is no greater tragedy in Christendom than spoiling children. If we want to help Christendom, we most certainly have to start with the children, as happened in earlier times.

"A Sermon on the Estate of Marriage" (1519)
LW 44, 12–13

Children

Wednesday

Pray in the Spirit at all times in every prayer and supplication. To that end keep alert and always persevere in supplication for all the saints.   Ephesians 6:18

You have needs enough: You are lacking in faith, in love, in patience, in gentleness, in chastity; my wife, my children are sick. Then pray undauntedly and with sure confidence, because God has commanded you to pray. He did not command it in order to deceive you and make a fool of you. He wants you to pray and to be confident that you will be heard; he wants you to open your bosom that he may give to you. But you must present your need to God, not the need of which you are not aware, but in order that you may learn to know yourself, where you are lacking, and to receive more and more the longer you hold open your sack.

Therefore, children right from the cradle on should begin to pray for the princes, for their brethren and companions. For here you hear the command and the promise: "Ask, and it will be given you; seek and you will find; knock, and it will be opened to you" (Matt. 7:7). You have been commanded to pray and promised that what you pray for will be given, as in Ps. 50:15, "Call upon me in the day of trouble; I will deliver you, and you shall glorify me"; and Ps. 91:15, "When he calls to me, I will answer him." So, go on that and say: Now I know that my prayer is not to be despised; for if I despise it, I despise the command and the promise of God. But God does not despise prayer, but rather has commanded it and promised that he will hear it.

"Ten Sermons on the Catechism" (1528)
LW 51, 171–72

For the unbelieving husband is made holy through his wife, and the unbelieving wife is made holy through her husband. Otherwise, your children would be unclean, but as it is, they are holy.
1 Corinthians 7:14

Thursday

St. Paul also wants to convey this: If a Christian spouse should have grown children with a non-Christian mate (as often happened in those days) and the children should not want to be baptized or become Christians, then, inasmuch as no one should be forced to believe but only willingly be drawn by God through His Gospel, the father and mother should not abandon the children or withdraw or fail in their motherly or fatherly duties, as though they could thereby sin and pollute themselves in unbelieving children. Rather they should guide and care bodily for these children as though they were the holiest of Christians. For they are not impure or unholy, Paul says; that is, your faith can demonstrate itself in them and thus remain pure and holy.

So it should be done now and at all times. Where children do not want to accept the Gospel, one should not therefore leave them or send them away but care for them and support them like the best of all Christians, commending their faith to God, so long as they are obedient and upright in all other things having to do with outward living. For parents can and should resist and punish outward evil acts and works. But nobody can resist and punish unbelief and an inwardly evil nature except God alone. Thus this text of St. Paul's also concerns us and strengthens us, making all things holy and pure to the believer.

"Commentary on 1 Corinthians 7" (1523)
LW 28, 35–36

Children

Friday

Now Esau hated Jacob because of the blessing with which his father had blessed him, and Esau said to himself, "The days of mourning for my father are approaching; then I will kill my brother Jacob."
Genesis 27:41

Let us recognize this great malice of the DEVIL. It is because of this malice that he has his own children in the homes of the saintliest people. They plot against the lives of their brothers and their own parents. Isaac is a very saintly patriarch, the father of the promise; Rebecca is a very saintly woman and the mother of the same promise. But Esau was born from their flesh and blood. He longs for their death, and he himself plans to bring it about. Of what will we not have to be afraid?

But the grief of parents is far more piercing and far bitterer than that of children, than that of brothers or relatives. For there are very great and intense emotions that God has created in the whole nature of things and has implanted in parents toward their offspring. And if at any time their hearts are wounded by grief or sorrow on account of a misfortune suffered by their children, this is a very real plague and a poison for their lives. Therefore parents are easily killed, if not by the sword, then by sorrow and grief. I myself have seen that many very honorable parents were slain by godless children because of sadness of heart. Young people neither consider nor understand this. But children should be taught and warned, lest they become murderers of mothers and murderers of fathers.

Lectures on Genesis (1541–42)
LW 5, 163–64

COMFORT

May the same Lord Jesus, who calls upon us to comfort one another, and who himself comforts us with his holy Word, comfort and strengthen your heart in steadfast patience by his Spirit until the happy end of this and all misfortune. To him, with the Father and the Holy Ghost, be honor and praise forever. Amen.

Letters, 227

Comfort

Monday

[The LORD] shielded him, cared for him,
guarded him as the apple of his eye.
Deuteronomy 32:10b

Never do we feel the hand of God more closely upon us than when we remember the years of our past life. St. Augustine says, "If people were given the choice between dying and reliving their past life, they would surely choose death, seeing the great dangers and evils which they had so narrowly escaped." When considered rightly, this statement is very true.

Here people may see how often they have done and suffered many things without effort or care of their own, yes, even without or against their own will. They gave little thought to them before they occurred or while they were happening. Only after all was over did they find themselves compelled to exclaim in great surprise, "How did these things happen to me, when I gave no thought to them, or thought something very different?" This bears out the proverb, "The human mind proposes, but God disposes" (Prov. 16:9). That is, God turns things around and brings to pass something different from that which people had planned. Thus it is not possible for us to deny that our lives and actions are under the guidance, not of our prudence, but of the wonderful power, wisdom, and goodness of God. Here we see how often God was with us when we neither saw nor sensed it.

Therefore, even if there were no books or sermons, our very own lives, led through so many evils and dangers, would, if considered properly, abundantly commend to us the ever present and most tender goodness of God, which, far beyond our thought and feeling, carried us in its bosom.

"Fourteen Consolations" (1520)
LW 42, 130–31

Comfort

Hide me in the shadow of your wings.
Psalm 17:8b

Tuesday

The shadow of your wings in a mystical sense is faith in Christ, which in this life is mysterious and shadowy. But the wings of Christ are His hands stretched out on the cross. For just as the body of Christ on the cross produces a shadow, so it casts a spiritual shadow on the soul, namely faith in His cross, under which every saint is protected.

Second, the shadow of the wings is the protection and watch of the holy angels or of contemplative people, who are the wings of God, for in them He soars and dwells in affectionate and encaptured minds.

Third, the shadow of the wings is the learning of the Scriptures, in which there is rest for those who devote themselves to this learning. Thus the bride says in Song of Sol. 2:3: "I sat down under his shadow, whom I desired."

First Lectures on the Psalms I (1513–15)
LW 10, 111

Wednesday
You are the most handsome of men; grace is poured upon your lips.   Psalm 45:2a

The poet has diligently read the prophecies and promises regarding Christ. He has seen that Christ's lips are the sweetest and loveliest lips, which attract the hearts of all the weak.

He does not call them simply "gracious" lips, but lips "overflowing with grace," in order to point out that Christ is superabundant in His lips. From His mouth, as from some overflowing fountain, the richest promises and teachings stem, and with these He strengthens and comforts souls.

Grace is on the lips of this King. Not only that, it overflows, so that you may understand how abundantly this fountain of grace flows and gushes forth. It is as though the psalmist said: "Our King has wisdom such as no one has, namely, the sweetest and loveliest wisdom. He helps the penitent, comforts the afflicted, recalls the despairing, raises up the fallen and humiliated, justifies sinners, gives life to the dying."

Christ Himself says in Isaiah 50:4: "The Lord has given Me the tongue of those who are taught, that I may know how to sustain with a word the one that is weary."

So mark this well. The tongue of Christ is not the kind that terrifies or hurts, except when He speaks to the proud and obstinate. This psalm speaks of the work which He exercises toward His own. Here nothing is heard but the voice of comfort for the lowly, the voice of joy, and the voice of the bridegroom.

Commentary on "Psalm 45" (1532)
LW 12, 211–12

Trust in him at all times, O people; pour out your heart before him; God is a refuge for us. Psalm 62:8

Thursday

Hope in God, for He will not let you down. Others laugh, comfort, and make promises, but do not pin your hopes on them. Do not depend on them, for both their strength and their courage are uncertain. Strength fades, courage fails; God remains firm. In times of adversity and in times of prosperity, therefore, you may depend on God.

If you are lacking something, well, here is good advice: "Pour out your heart before Him." Voice your complaint freely, and do not conceal anything from Him. Regardless of what it is, just throw it in a pile before Him, as you open your heart completely to a good friend. He wants to hear it, and He wants to give you His aid and counsel. Do not be bashful before Him and do not think that what you ask is too big or too much. Come right out with it, even if all you have is bags full of need. Out with everything; God is greater and more able and more willing than all our transgressions. Do not dribble your requests before Him; God is not a person whom you can overburden with your begging and asking. The more you ask, the happier He is to hear you. Only pour it all out, do not dribble or drip it. For He will not drip or dribble either, for He will flood you with a veritable deluge.

"God is a Refuge for us," our Hiding Place, He and no one else.

Commentary on "The Four Psalms of Comfort" (1526)
LW 14, 237–38

Friday

"Do not let your hearts be troubled."
John 14:1a

Christ knows that if we want to remain His own and adhere to Baptism, the Sacrament, and the Gospel, the devil will inevitably be our enemy, incessantly pressing us with all his might and contending for our body and soul. Even if God wards him off and prevents him from killing you in one day, he will nevertheless craftily and cunningly persist in trying at least to rob you of your courage and security. He will try to fill you with disquietude and sadness, and subsequently to bring you into other dangers and distress. Christ here wants to exhort and console us, that we may be reconciled to our lot and not be too alarmed or let the devil subdue us so easily and make us despair and lose courage.

From these and similar words of Christ we should learn to know the Lord Christ aright, to develop a more cordial and comforting confidence in Him. We are to learn to pay more regard to His Word than to anything else which may confront our eyes, ears, and other senses.

For if I am a Christian and hold to Him, I always know that He is talking to me. Here and elsewhere I learn that all His words are intended to comfort me. Yes, all He says, does and thinks are nothing but friendly and consoling words and works. To this end He promises to send His disciples and the Christians the Holy Spirit, whom He calls the Comforter.

Sermons on the Gospel of St. John (1537)
LW 24, 12–13

HEARING GOD

O dear Lord, Father and God, keep us fit and alert, eager and diligent in your word and service, so that we do not become complacent, lazy, and slothful as though we had already achieved everything. In that way the fearful devil cannot fall upon us, surprise us, and deprive us of your precious word or stir up strife and factions among us and lead us into other sin and disgrace, both spiritually and physically. Rather grant us wisdom and strength through your spirit that we may valiantly resist him and gain the victory. Amen.

LW 43, 197

Hearing God

Monday

*But their delight is in the law of the
LORD, and on his law they meditate day
and night.   Psalm 1:2*

This delight or desire comes from faith in God through Jesus Christ. On the other hand, a desire which has been extorted through fear of punishment is servile and impetuous, while that which is induced through a desire for reward is mercenary and false. But this person's desire is free; it does not seek reward and is happy. It becomes clear then that if this psalm is not understood of Christ alone, it becomes a mirror and a goal toward which the blessed person must strive.

But through this desire the believer has become one with the Word of God as love unites the lover with the beloved. And the desire is the whole life of that person for wherever love goes, there the heart and the body follow. Here we are able to see the contrasting life of the pious and the impious. The ungodly begin their righteousness from the outside and proceed inward. First they pretend works, then words, and only afterwards do they practice thinking. This is the greatest height they reach. Then they soon become masters of others. They insist that all they think, do, and say, is holy and divine, although they never arrive at the hidden will.

The godly, on the other hand, begin from the inside. They start with this holy desire, and then follow meditation and external works, and after this the teaching of others. For it is the mode and nature of all who love, to chatter, sing, think, compose, and frolic freely about what they love and to enjoy hearing about it. Therefore this lover, this blessed person, has this love, the Law of God, always in the mouth, always in the heart and, if possible, always in the ear. "Whoever is of God hears the words of God" (John 8:47).

"Psalm 1" (1519–21)
LW 14, 295, 297–98

And when he had finished talking with **Tuesday**
him, God went up from Abraham.
Genesis 17:22

It is indeed something very great to have God conversing and associating with us. Even though God does not appear to us in an extraordinary form as He did to Abraham, yet His usual and most friendly and most intimate appearance is this, that He presents Himself to us in the Word, in Baptism, in the Lord's Supper, and in the use of the Keys [God's spiritual power given to the Christian Church to distribute the blessings of the Gospel (Matt. 18:18)].

These facts must be impressed rather frequently, and it is not without reason that I am repeating them. If Abraham should be compared with us who live in the New Testament, he is, for the most part, less important than we are, provided that one considers the matter impartially. To be sure, in his case the personal gifts are greater; but God did not manifest Himself to him in a closer and more friendly manner than He does to us. Let it indeed be a great glory to have those appearances, but what greater or better advantage did Abraham have from them than the fact that God spoke with him?

This happens to us too, and indeed daily, as often as and where ever we wish. It is true that you hear a human being when you are baptized and when you partake of the Holy Supper. But the Word which you hear is not that of a human being; it is the Word of the living God. It is He who baptizes you. It is He who absolves you from sins. It is He who commands you to hope in His mercy.

Lectures on Genesis (1538)
LW 3, 165–66

Wednesday

Anyone who resolves to do the will of God will know whether the teaching is from God.   John 7:17a

Now this is the will of the Father, that we be intent on hearing what the Man Christ has to say, that we listen to His Word. You must not quibble at His Word, find fault with it, and dispute it. Just hear it.

Then the Holy Spirit will come and prepare your heart, that you may sincerely believe the preaching of the divine Word, even give up your life for it, and say: "This is God's Word and the pure truth." But if you insist that you be heard, that your reason interpret Christ's Word; if you presume to play the master of the Word, to propound other doctrines, if you probe it, measure it, and twist the words to read as you want them to, brood over them, hesitate, doubt, and then judge them according to your reason—that is not hearing the Word or being its pupil. Then you are setting yourself up as its schoolmaster. In that way you will never discover the meaning of Christ's Word or of His heavenly Father's will.

Simply hear what the Son of God says. Hear His word, and adhere to it. It is written: "Hear Him!" To hear, to hear—that is the command, and thus we truly conform to God's will. He has promised to give the Holy Spirit to anyone who hears the Son, to enlighten and inflame one to understand that it is God's Word. God will make a believer out of each one after His own heart. This He will surely do.

Sermons on the Gospel of St. John (1530–32)
LW 23, 229–30

"How beautiful are the feet of those who bring good news!" Romans 10:15b

Thursday

In the first place, they are called "beautiful" because of their purity, since they do not preach the Gospel for personal advantage or empty glory, but only out of obedience to God as well as for the salvation of the hearers.

In the second place, the term "beautiful" according to the Hebrew idiom has more the meaning of something desirable or hoped for, something favored or worthy of love and affection. Thus the meaning is that the preaching of the Gospel is something lovable and desirable for those who are under the Law.

But what is meant by the term "feet"? According to the first interpretation the term refers to the attitude and the devotion of those who preach, which must be free of all love of money and glory.

But according to the Hebrew, which is more accurate, the term "feet" can be taken in a literal sense, namely, that the coming of preachers of good things is something desirable for those who are tortured by sins and an evil conscience. And even more correctly the term can signify their very words themselves or the sound and the syllables, the pronunciation of the words of those who preach. For their voices are like feet or vehicles or wheels by which the Word is carried or rolled or it walks to the ears of the hearers. Hence he says: "Their voice goes out through all the earth" (Ps. 19:4). And again: "His Word runs swiftly" (Ps. 147:15). Whatever runs has feet: the Word runs, therefore the Word has feet, which are its pronunciations and its sounds. While the hearer sits quietly and receives the Word, the "feet" of the preacher run over him.

Lectures on Romans (1515–16)
LW 25, 415–17

Friday

Therefore, as the Holy Spirit says: "Today, if you hear his voice, do not harden your hearts." Hebrews 3:7-8a

One should note that this is the one, and the greatest, thing God requires of all people, that they hear His voice. Therefore Moses impresses so many times throughout Deuteronomy: "Hear, O Israel" and "If you hear the voice of the Lord your God." Indeed, nothing resounds in the prophets more frequently than "hear," "they did not hear," and "they were unwilling to hear." And rightly so, because without faith it is impossible for God to be with us (cf. Heb. 11:6), or to work, since He does everything through His Word alone. Thus none are able to cooperate with Him unless they adhere to the Word.

But human nature recoils violently from this hearing. Therefore, those who rely on their own counsel and "do not wait for the counsel of the Lord" (cf. Ps. 106:13) harden their hearts to their own immeasurable harm and impede the work of God in themselves. For God works beyond strength, beyond perception, beyond intention, and beyond every thought.

From this one now understands who the people are who annoy, irritate, exasperate, and contradict, as Scripture rather frequently speaks of them, namely, the people who do not believe the Word of God and are impatient of the work of God. They follow their master as long as they are aware of visible things to rely on. If these things fail, they fail too. Therefore faith in Christ is an exceedingly arduous thing. It is a removal from everything one experiences within and without to the things one experiences neither within nor without, namely to the invisible, most high, and incomprehensible God.

"Lectures on Hebrews" (1517–18)
LW 29, 148–49

HOPE

Almighty, everlasting God, whose Son has assured forgiveness of sins and deliverance from eternal death, strengthen us by your Holy Spirit that our faith in Christ increase daily and we hold fast the hope that we shall not die but fall asleep and on the last day be raised to eternal life; through Jesus Christ, our Lord. Amen.

Lutheran Worship, 126, #120

Monday

For through the Spirit, by faith, we eagerly wait for the hope of righteousness.
Galatians 5:5

Therefore when I take hold of Christ as I have been taught by faith in the Word of God, and when I believe in Him with the full confidence of my heart—something that cannot happen without the will—then I am righteous through this knowledge. When I have been thus justified by faith or by this knowledge, then immediately the devil comes and exerts himself to extinguish my faith with his tricks, his lies, errors and heresies, violence, tyranny, and murder.

Then my battling hope grasps what faith has commanded; it becomes vigorous and conquers the devil, who attacks faith. When he has been conquered, there follow peace and joy in the Holy Spirit. Faith and hope are scarcely distinguishable; and yet there is some difference between them.

Therefore faith is like dialectic, which conceives the idea of all the things that are to be believed; and hope is like rhetoric, which develops, urges, persuades, and exhorts to steadiness, so that faith does not collapse in temptation but keeps the Word and holds firmly to it.

Lectures on Galatians (1535)
LW 27, 23–24

Hoping against hope, [Abraham] believed that he would become "the father of many nations." Romans 4:18

Tuesday

Truly devout people have nothing dearer and more precious in the whole world than this doctrine. Those who hold to this know what the whole world does not know, namely, that sin and death, as well as other calamities and evils, both physical and spiritual, work out for the good of the elect. They also know that God is present most closely when He seems to be farthest away, and that He is most merciful and most the Savior when He seems most to be wrathful and to punish and condemn. They know that they have eternal righteousness, for which they look in hope as an utterly certain possession [Gal. 5:5], laid up in heaven, when they are most aware of the terrors of sin and death; and that they are the lords of everything when they seem to be the poorest of all, according to the words, "as having nothing, and yet possessing everything" (2 Cor. 6:10). This is what Scripture calls gaining comfort through hope. But this art is not learned without frequent and great trials.

Lectures on Galatians (1535)
LW 27, 27

Wednesday

The saying is sure and worthy of full acceptance. For to this end we toil and struggle, because we have our hope set on the living God, who is the Savior of all people, especially of those who believe.
1 Timothy 4:9-10

This firm hope which we have makes us quick to work and to bear reproach. This statement is sure because we have this Man who will yet come. So we work, exercise godliness, do our tasks, observe all things, that the glory of God may grow and the kingdom of God may be spread.

As to our hardships: then we not only work but also suffer. In both areas we practice the Word, actively and passively. Why this? Because our hope rests on a living God. We do not place our hope in the world. We do not work or suffer reproach so that we experience the favor, wealth, and high positions of the world. We do not hope in an imaginary god. Such are the gods of hypocrites, who make up gods for themselves with their false religion. They work and suffer in vain, because their hopes lie in an imaginary god.

Our hope truly is in a real God. Those who hope in God know for certain that their works and suffering please God. They most certainly experience mercy and grace from God. The person, then, who has this confidence acts the more freely and endures everything, because he or she always has this confidence in pleasing God.

"Lectures on 1 Timothy" (1527–28)
LW 28, 325

"And I will put enmity between you and the woman, and between your offspring and hers; he will strike your head, and you will strike his heel." Genesis 3:15

Thursday

This is the text that made Adam and Eve alive and brought them back from death into the life which they had lost through sin. Nevertheless, the life is one hoped for rather than one already possessed. Similarly, Paul also often says (1 Cor. 15:31): "Daily we die." Although we do not wish to call the life we live here a death, nevertheless it surely is nothing else than a continuous journey toward death. Just as a person infected with a plague has already started to die when the infection has begun, so—because of sin, and death, the punishment for sin—this life can no longer properly be called life after it has been infected by sin. Right from our mother's womb we begin to die.

Through Baptism we are restored to a life of hope, or rather to a hope of life. This is the true life, which is lived before God. Before we come to it, we are in the midst of death. We die and decay in the earth, just as other dead bodies do, as though there were no other life anywhere. Yet we who believe in Christ have the hope that on the Last Day we shall be revived for eternal life.

Lectures on Genesis (1535–36)
LW 1, 196

Friday

A broken and contrite heart, O God, you will not despise.   Psalm 51:17b

This is a description of God that is full of comfort: that in His true form God is a God who loves the afflicted, has mercy upon the humbled, forgives the fallen, and revives the drooping. How can any more pleasant picture be painted of God? This verse rejects all other acts of worship and all works and simply calls us back to trust alone in the mercy and kindness of God, so that we believe that God is favorably disposed to us even when we seem to ourselves to be forsaken and distressed.

Thus when Nathan denounced David (2 Sam. 12:7): "You are that man of death," David was humbled and undertook this sacrifice. Then when he heard (2 Sam. 12:13): "You shall not die," he completed the sacrifice. In the midst of wrath he acquired hope in mercy; in the midst of a feeling of death he acquired a hope in life. From that experience this verse was born, by which we are taught about a sacrifice acceptable to God, namely, to hope for life and grace amid death and the wrath of God.

This theology must be learned through experience. Without experience it cannot be understood that the "poor in spirit" (Matt. 5:3) should know that they are in grace when they most feel the wrath of God, that in despair they should keep their hope in mercy, and in smugness they should keep their fear of God. As another passage says (Ps. 147:11): "The Lord takes pleasure in those who fear Him, in those who hope in His steadfast love."

Commentary on "Psalm 51" (1532)
LW 12, 406

MUSIC

Grant, O Lord God, that what we have heard with our ears and sung with our lips, we may believe in our hearts and practice in our lives; for Jesus Christ's sake. Amen.

Minister's Prayer Book, 145, #234 (Traditional)

Monday

By the streams the birds of the air have their habitation; they sing among the branches.   Psalm 104:12

Greetings in Christ! I would certainly like to praise music with all my heart as the excellent gift of God which it is and to commend it to everyone. But I am so overwhelmed by the diversity and magnitude of its virtue and benefits that I can find neither beginning nor end or method for my discourse. As much as I want to commend it, my praise is bound to be wanting and inadequate. For who can comprehend it all? And even if you wanted to encompass all of it, you would appear to have grasped nothing at all.

First then, looking at music itself, you will find that from the beginning of the world it has been instilled and implanted in all creatures, individually and collectively. For nothing is without sound or harmony. Even the air, which of itself is invisible and imperceptible to all our senses, and which, since it lacks both voice and speech, is the least musical of all things, becomes sonorous, audible, and comprehensible when it is set in motion. Wondrous mysteries are here suggested by the Spirit, but this is not the place to dwell on them. Music is still more wonderful in living things, especially birds, so that David, the most musical of all the kings and minstrel of God, in deepest wonder and spiritual exultation praised the astounding art and ease of the song of the birds.

And yet, compared to the human voice, all this hardly deserves the name music, so abundant and incomprehensible is here the munificence and wisdom of our most gracious Creator.

"Preface to Georg Rhau's Symphoniae Iucundae" (1538)
LW 53, 321–22

David took the lyre and played it with his hand, and Saul would be relieved and feel better, and the evil spirit would depart from him.   *1 Samuel 16:23*

Tuesday

Here it must suffice to discuss the benefit of this great art. He can mention only one point (which experience confirms), namely, that next to the Word of God, music deserves the highest praise. She is a mistress and governess of those human emotions which, as masters, govern mortals or more often overwhelm them. No greater commendation than this can be found—at least not by us. For whether you wish to comfort the sad, to terrify the happy, to encourage the despairing, to humble the proud, to calm the passionate, or to appease those full of hate—and who could number all the masters of the human heart, namely, the emotions, inclinations, and affections that impel people to evil or good?—what more effective means than music could you find?

The Holy Ghost himself honors music as an instrument for his proper work when in his Holy Scriptures he asserts that through her his gifts were instilled in the prophets, namely, the inclination to all virtues, as can be seen in Elisha (2 Kings 3:15). On the other hand, she serves to cast out Satan, the instigator of all sins, as is shown in Saul, the king of Israel (1 Sam. 16:23).

"Preface to Georg Rhau's Symphoniae Iucundae" (1538)
LW 53, 323

Wednesday

It is good to give thanks to the LORD, to sing praises to your name, O Most High; to declare your steadfast love in the morning, and your faithfulness by night, to the music of the lute and the harp, to the melody of the lyre.   Psalm 92:1-3

Thus it was not without reason that the forebears and prophets wanted nothing else to be associated as closely with the Word of God as music. Therefore, we have so many hymns and Psalms where message and music join to move the listener's soul, while in other living beings and sounding bodies music remains a language without words. After all, the gift of language combined with the gift of song was only given to us to let us know that we should praise God with both words and music, namely, by proclaiming the Word of God through music and by providing sweet melodies with words.

But the subject is much too great for me briefly to describe all its benefits. And you, my young friend, let this noble, wholesome, and cheerful creation of God be commended to you. By it you may escape shameful desires and bad company. At the same time you may by this creation accustom yourself to recognize and praise the Creator. Take special care to shun perverted minds who prostitute this lovely gift of nature and of art with their erotic rantings. Be quite assured that none but the devil goads them on to defy their very nature which would and should praise God its Maker with this gift, so that these scoundrels purloin the gift of God and use it to worship the foe of God, the enemy of nature and of this lovely art.

"Preface to Georg Rhau's Symphoniae Iucundae" (1538)
LW 53, 323–24

O sing to the LORD *a new song.*
Psalm 96:1a

Thursday

The psalm says, "Sing to the Lord a new song. Sing to the Lord all the earth." For in the Old Covenant under the law of Moses, divine service was tedious and tiresome as the people had to offer so many and varied sacrifices of all they possessed, both in house and field. And since they were restive and selfish, they performed this service unwillingly or only for the sake of temporal gain. As the prophet Malachi asks, "Who is there even among you that would shut the doors for nought or kindle a light on my altar for nothing?" [Mal. 1:10] Now with a heart as lazy and unwilling as this, nothing or nothing good can be sung. Heart and mind must be cheerful and willing if one is to sing. Therefore, God abrogated the service that was rendered so indolently and reluctantly.

Thus there is not in the New Testament a better service of God, of which the psalm here says: "Sing to the Lord a new song." For God has cheered our hearts and minds through his dear Son, whom he gave for us to redeem us from sin, death, and the devil. Those who believe this earnestly cannot be quiet about it. But they must gladly and willingly sing and speak about it so that others also may come and hear it. And those who do not want to sing and speak of it show that they do not believe and that they do not belong under the new and joyful testament, but under the old, lazy, and tedious testament.

Therefore, the printers do well if they publish a lot of good hymns and make them attractive to the people with all sorts of ornamentations, so that they may move them to joy in faith and to gladly sing.

"Preface to the Babst Hymnal" (1545)
LW 53, 332–33

Music

Friday

These are the last words of David: "The oracle of David, the son of Jesse, the oracle of the man who is assured of the Messiah of the God of Jacob, the sweet psalmist of Israel."
2 Samuel 23:1-2 (Luther's translation)

When David uses the word *sweet* he is not thinking only of the sweetness and the charm of the Psalms from a grammatical and musical point of view, of artistic and euphonious words, of melodious songs and notes, of beautiful text and beautiful tune. He is referring much more to the theology they contain, to the spiritual meaning. That renders the Psalms lovely and sweet, for they are a solace to all saddened and wretched consciences, ensnared in the fear of sin, in the torture and terror of death, and in all sorts of adversity and misery. To such hearts the Book of Psalms is a sweet and delightful song because it sings of and proclaims the Messiah even when a person does not sing the notes but merely recites and pronounces the words. And yet the music, or the notes, which are a wonderful creation and gift of God, help materially in this, especially when the people sing along and reverently participate. For the evil spirit is ill at ease wherever God's Word is sung or preached in true faith. He is a spirit of gloom and cannot abide where he finds a spiritually happy heart, that is, where the heart rejoices in God and in His Word.

"Treatise on the Last Words of David (2 Sam. 23:1-7)" (1543)
LW 15, 273–74

THANKFULNESS

Lord God, heavenly Father, from whom without ceasing we receive exceedingly abundantly all good gifts and by whom we are guarded daily from every evil: Grant us we beseech you by your Spirit that we in true faith may acknowledge your goodness with our whole heart and may now and evermore thank and praise your loving-kindness and tender mercy; through Jesus Christ your Son our Lord. Amen.

LW 53, 139

Monday

He journeyed on by stages from the Negeb as far as Bethel, to the place where his tent had been at the beginning, between Bethel and Ai, to the place where he had made an altar at the first; and there Abram called on the name of the LORD.
Genesis 13:3-4

It is impossible to pray unless one has first instructed the people concerning God. In fact, you will never pray successfully in private unless you have preached to yourself either the Creed or some other passage of Scripture that draws your attention to the goodness of God as the One who has not only commanded you to pray but has also added the promise that He will hear you. Through this private sermon, which you direct to yourself, your heart is impelled to pray.

The same thing takes place publicly in our churches. We have no silent forms of worship, but the voice of the Gospel is always heard. Through it people are taught about the will of God. And to the sermons we add prayers or thanksgivings.

Moreover, Abraham is praised in this passage because he did these things, not in some corner—for fear of the threats or the violence of the heathen—but in a public place, in order that by his own example and that of his people he might lead others to the knowledge of God and to true forms of worship.

Lectures on Genesis (ca. 1536)
LW 2, 333

Answer me when I call, O God of my   **Tuesday**
right! You gave me room when I was in
distress.   *Psalm 4:1*

The best way to lift the mind up to God is to acknowledge and ponder past blessings. The setting forth of past blessings is the guarantee of future ones, and gifts received in the past offer the confidence of receiving them. On the contrary, the total sinking of the mind away from God down to hell consists in forgetting or failing to take note of goods received.

Therefore, one must begin with thanksgiving and confession. The psalmist takes note of the good things received in prosperity and the good things received in adversity. He reflects upon both in brief words but in very broad thoughts.

See how true and godly is this confession, in which he arrogates nothing of merit to himself. He does not say, "Since I did much or earned much in deed or with the mouth or some other member of mine." He lays claim to no righteousness, he boasts of no merit, he displays no worth, but he praises the pure and exclusive grace and free kindness of God. He finds nothing within himself on the basis of which God should answer him. He only prays and keeps everything else quiet. Such a person "appears empty before the Lord" in the best way, because the person is empty for [self] but full for God.

First Lectures on the Psalms I (1513–15)
LW 10, 45–46

Wednesday

Then you will delight in right sacrifices, in burnt offerings and whole burnt offerings; then bulls will be offered on your altar.
Psalm 51:19

You can understand all the sacrifices correctly—those that were done according to the Law and spiritual sacrifices. Both are sacrifices of righteousness, because their whole power is in the goodness of God and in divine blessing. When people trust in mercy this way, then if an ox is offered, it pleases God and is a sacrifice of righteousness. If there is no ox, then the "ox of our lips," as Hosea calls it (Hos. 14:2) pleases Him. This is the way I interpret all sacrifices. They are called sacrifices of righteousness, not because they justify but because they are done by those who are justified or righteous. Because the people are righteous and know that they please God by grace alone, not by some worthiness or merits of their own, whatever they do according to the Word of God is truly called either a sacrifice or a work of righteousness.

In the psalm David sets forth a double sacrifice. The first is what he calls "a contrite heart." This is the first and most powerful sacrifice. After you have thus acknowledged God to be the Justifier of sinners, if you sing God even one song of thanks, you add another sacrifice, namely a sacrifice of thanksgiving for the gift you have received. This sacrifice is not merit but a confession and testimony of the grace which your God has bestowed upon you out of sheer mercy.

Thus the saints and the righteous in the Old Testament brought burnt offerings with the purpose not of being justified through them, but of testifying that they had received mercy and comfort.

Commentary on "Psalm 51" (1532)
LW 12, 408–9

They will be called oaks of righteousness, the planting of the LORD, to display his glory.   Isaiah 61:3c

Thursday

It is as if God said: "I will dress my Christians up as a paradise of righteousnesses, *that they may be called oaks of righteousness, the planting of the Lord.* They shall grow for Me in spite of the world's disapproval." Here the prophet describes a garden that is planted by God and continues to grow. All the trees of this garden are called righteous. In the world there are also very large trees like the cedars, but they are trees of unrighteousness and iniquity. But in this garden they will be righteous, planted by God. Thus it follows that a Christian does not just come into being, but is planted and produced by the work of God and Christ is the gardener. For through the Word one is uprooted from the world and transplanted into this garden and watered. In this way the prophet comforts himself and sets before himself Christianity as a most beautiful garden.

And then he states the reason—*that He may be glorified.* This is our work, to praise and give thanks to God. It is as if he said: "In this garden there will be nothing, no ceremonies of the Law and no sacrifices, except a single fruit from the trees—glorification, praise, and thanksgiving." The letters will stand on all the leaves. What lovely trees they are, having "thanksgiving" imprinted on them!

Lectures on Isaiah (1527–30)
LW 17, 336

Friday

I will recount the gracious deeds of the Lord, the praiseworthy acts of the LORD, because of all that the LORD has done for us.   Isaiah 63:7a

Now the prophet sings a song and gathers the praises into a poem. In all of Scripture it is customary for all the saints and prophets to console themselves in times of trial by recalling past benefits.

And he is not speaking of just one benefit. He wants to embrace all of them. This is not a mean art but the art of the Holy Spirit. Reason cannot sing about the Lord's blessings. It is the work of the Spirit alone to understand the mercies of the Lord. It is the wise person who begins to praise and give thanks. Reason of itself cannot do this. It only observes the threats and terrors of God and the ungodliness of the world, and then it begins to murmur and blaspheme. Why? Because the flesh cannot enumerate the blessings; it lists only the bad things and not the good things. Reason sees the world as extremely ungodly, and therefore it murmurs. The Spirit sees nothing but God's benefits in the world and therefore begins to sing. This calls for wisdom.

Lectures on Isaiah (1527–30)
LW 17, 355–56

CHRIST THE KING

Almighty God, who by the death of your Son has brought to naught sin and death and by his resurrection has brought again innocence and everlasting life so that, delivered from the devil's power, we may live in your Kingdom: Grant us that we may believe this with all our heart and, steadfast in this faith, praise and thank you always; through the same your Son Jesus Christ our Lord. Amen.

LW 53, 134

Christic the King

Monday

The LORD says to my lord, "Sit at my right hand."   *Psalm 110:1a*

One word exalts Him to the position of a glorious King! Not over that beggarly palace in Jerusalem or the imperial throne of Babylon, or Rome, or Constantinople, or the whole earth—which would indeed represent tremendous power. Not merely king of the heavens, the stars, and anything else that the eye can see! This is something far higher and more important, for it means: "Sit next to Me on the exalted throne upon which I sit, and be My equal!"

To sit next to Him—at His right hand, not at His feet—means to possess the very majesty and power that is called divine. Surely, by this one short word Christ is raised from the earth and exalted above all the heavens, as St. Paul says (Phil. 2:9-10), and becomes a King inconceivably glorious and of unspeakable power. He is not merely a king who rules over all people, but one who is above the heavens, angels, and anything else that is subject to God.

Commentary on "Psalm 110" (1535)
LW 13, 233–34

[Jesus Christ] has gone into heaven and is at the right hand of God, with angels, authorities, and powers made subject to him.   1 Peter 3.22

Tuesday

This is really an extraordinary kingdom. This King sits above at the right hand of God, where He is invisible, an eternal, immortal Person. But His people are here below on earth in this miserable, mortal condition, subjected to death and any kind of mishap which a person may meet on earth.

But this Lord Christ sits above at the right hand of God, having a kingdom of life, peace, joy, and redemption from all evil, not a kingdom of death, sorrow, and misery. Therefore it must follow that His own will not remain subject to death, anxiety, fear, spiritual conflict, and suffering. They will be snatched from death or the grave and all misery. They will live with Him beyond sin and evil after He has made them alive again in body and soul.

He illustrates this in His own Person. He became a human being and condescended to the miserable level of our present nature in order to begin His kingdom in us by personally sharing all human weakness and trouble. For this reason He also had to die. But if He was meant to be Lord and King of all creation, sitting at the right hand of God, He could not remain under the conditions of death and suffering. By God's power He had to break through death and the grave and everything else, so that He might seat Himself at the place where He can work all these things in us and grant them to us.

Commentary on "Psalm 110" (1535)
LW 13, 240–41

Wednesday

"When he ascended on high he made captivity itself a captive; he gave gifts to his people." Ephesians 4:8b

Behold the glory of this King! It surpasses all that is glorious and powerful, whether in heaven or on earth. He is a different Lord, unlike those who have land and people, cities and castles, silver and gold, body and goods. He is Lord and King of eternal possessions that are peculiar to God, such as peace and joy and the immeasurable wealth of eternal righteousness and life. Of course, He also holds in His hands all that pertains to this temporal life, whatever there is of power and authority. He can do with it as He sees fit. Hence all princes and lords are subject to Him; they cannot reach beyond the limits He has set for them. But as Psalm 110 shows, it is of special importance that the devil, death, and sin have been put under His feet unconditionally.

At this point we must mention the faith that takes hold of the King. We must learn to see Christ thus and to believe it with certainty, so that He becomes such a Lord for us also. For He is not someone who lolls in heaven and has fun with the angels. He exercises His authority and government vigorously and under all conditions by controlling the hearts of all. He does truly govern, lead, save, protect, and preserve His Christendom. All who believe in Him and call upon Him certainly receive the gifts described by St. Paul, who cites Psalm 68:18 in Ephesians 4:8 to show that Christ ascended on high and seated Himself at the right hand of God in order to give people such divine gifts.

Commentary on "Psalm 110" (1535)
LW 13, 241

Your solemn processions are seen, O God, the processions of my God, my King, into the sanctuary.   Psalm 68:24

God's "processions" represent His work, which is steadfast love and faithfulness. Thus we read in Psalm 25:10: "All the paths of the Lord are steadfast love and faithfulness." However, it requires great skill to recognize God's work and to let Him work in us, so that all our work will in the end be God's and not our own. This is the proper celebration of the Sabbath, to rest from our own works and to be full of God's works. All this is effected in us through faith, which teaches that we count for naught and our work no less. This is what the psalmist has in mind when he says: "Thy processions are seen and recognized." And the words "my God, my King" point to Christ, who is our King according to His human nature and who is God from eternity.

We cannot say "My God and my King" unless we regard God with the eyes of faith, not only as a God, not only as a King, but as *our* God and *our* King, as the God and King of our salvation. Neither is it possible to recognize the ways and works of God in the absence of that faith. Faith renders Him my God and my King, and brings me to a realization that all my works are, after all, not mine but God's.

Commentary on "Psalm 68" (1521)
LW 13, 25–26

Friday

In your majesty ride forth victoriously in behalf of truth, humility and righteousness; let your right hand display awesome deeds.
Psalm 45:4 (NIV)

Therefore rouse yourself. Do not give in to evils, but go forth more boldly against them. Hold on. Do not be disheartened either by contempt or ingratitude within or by agitation and raging without. It is in sorrow, when we are the closest to despair, that hope rises the highest. So today, when there is the greatest contempt and weariness with the Word, the true glory of the Word begins.

Therefore we should learn to understand this verse as speaking of invisible progress and success. Our King enjoys success and good fortune even though you do not see it. Moreover, it would not be expedient for us to see this success, for then we would be puffed up. Now, however, He raises us up through faith and gives us hope. Even though we see no fruit of the Word, still we can be certain that fruit will not be wanting but will certainly follow. We should not be discouraged when we look at present circumstances that disturb us, but we should much rather look at Christ's promises. He is the kind of king who will have success, steadfastness, and victory—if not in this place and time, then at another time and place. This splendor and success is clearer than all the stars, even though we do not see it.

Commentary on "Psalm 45" (1532)
LW 12, 220–21

BIBLIOGRAPHY

Tappert, Theodore G., ed. and trans. *Luther: Letters of Spiritual Counsel.*
Vol. 18 of *The Library of Christian Classics.* Philadelphia: The West-
minster Press, 1955.

Lutheran Book of Worship. Minneapolis: Augsburg Publishing House,
1978.

The Lutheran Hymnal. St. Louis: Concordia Publishing House, 1941.

Lutheran Worship. St. Louis: Concordia Publishing House, 1982.

Pelikan, Jaroslav, and Helmut Lehmann, eds. *Luther's Works.* American
Edition. Philadelphia and St. Louis: Fortress Press and Concordia
Publishing House, 1955–1984.

Doberstein, John W., ed. *Minister's Prayer Book.* Philadelphia: Muhl-
enberg Press, n.d.

Plass, Ewald M., ed. *What Luther Says.* An Anthology. St. Louis:
Concordia Publishing House, 1959.

INDEX

Topical Index

Scriptural Index